KT-372-897

ST 015853

CORNWALL COLLEGE

THE DESIGNER'S
PACKAGING BIBLE

RotoVision

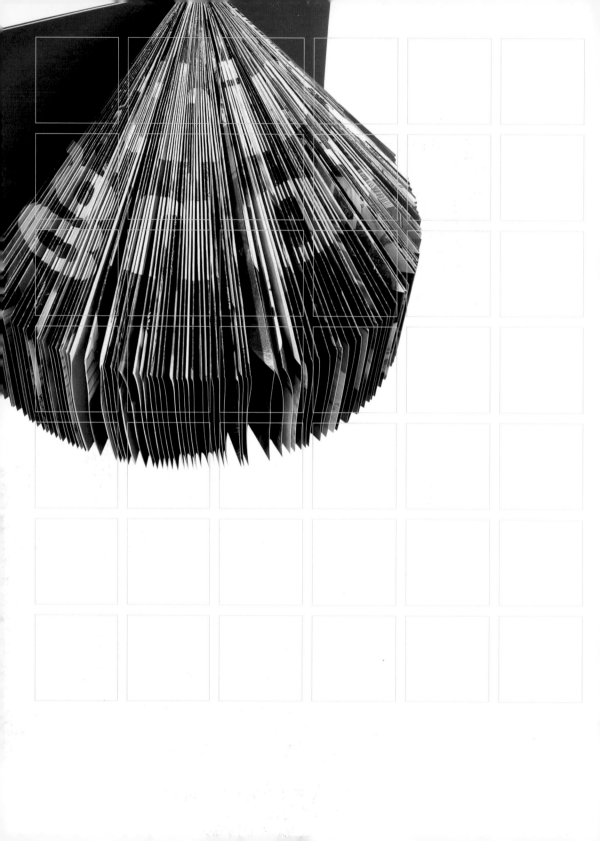

THE DESIGNER'S
PACKAGING BIBLE

CREATIVE SOLUTIONS FOR OUTSTANDING DESIGN

COMPILED BY
LUKE HERRIOTT

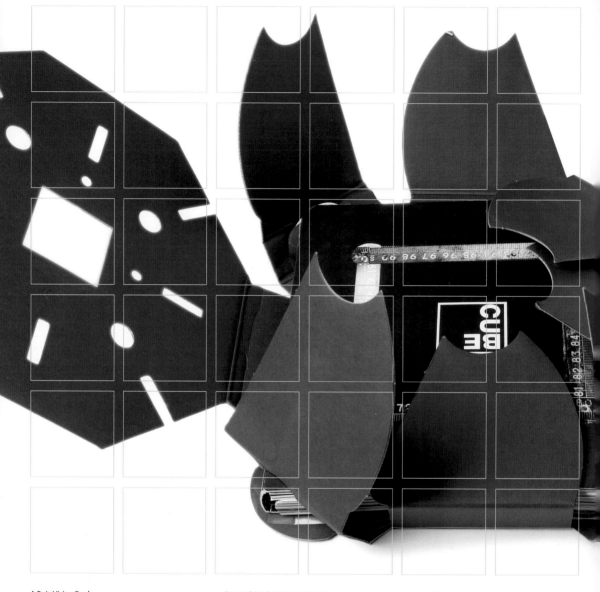

A RotoVision Book

Published and distributed by RotoVision SA
Route Suisse 9
CH-1295 Mies
Switzerland

RotoVision SA
Sales and Editorial Office
Sheridan House, 114 Western Road
Hove BN3 1DD, UK

Tel: +44 (0)1273 72 72 68
Fax: +44 (0)1273 72 72 69
www.rotovision.com

Copyright © RotoVision SA 2007

All rights reserved. No part of this publication may be
reproduced, stored in a retrieval system, or transmitted
in any form or by any means, electronic, mechanical,
photocopying, recording or otherwise, without
permission of the copyright holder.

While every effort has been made to contact owners
of copyright material produced in this book, we have
not always been successful. In the event of a
copyright query, please contact the Publisher.

10 9 8 7 6 5 4 3 2 1
ISBN: 978-2-940361-72-4

Art Director: Tony Seddon
Design by Studio Ink

Reprographics in Singapore by ProVision Pte.
Tel: +65 6334 7720
Fax: +65 6334 7721

Printed in China by Midas Printing International Ltd.

Learning Services
Cornwall College St Austell

Class	745.2 - HER
Barcode	ST015853
Date	00/08	Centre	SKH

CONTENTS

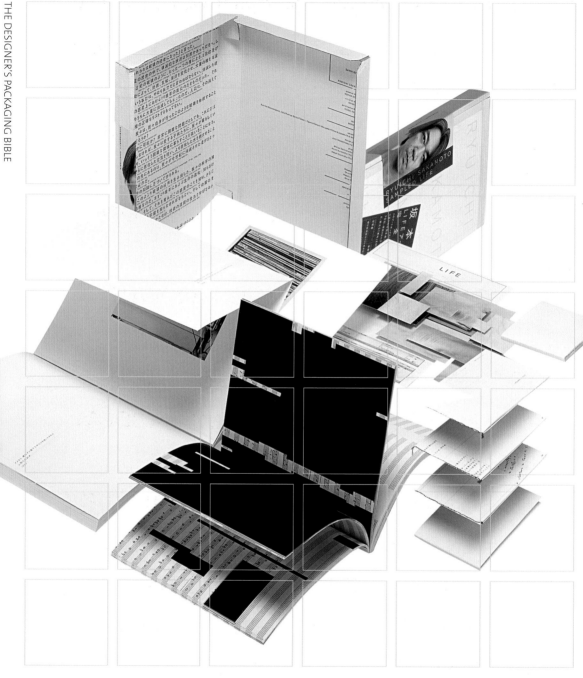

SPECIAL FEATURES KEY

 SPECIAL INK

 FOLDED

SPECIAL BINDING

DIE-CUT

 EMBOSSED

SPECIAL MATERIAL

 ADD-ON

 TEXT

INCLUDES BAGS, BOOKS, BROCHURES, CALENDARS, CATALOGS, CD PACKAGING, COMPANY REPORTS, DESIGN MANIFESTOS, DVD PACKAGING, FLYERS, GREETINGS CARDS, GIFTS, INVITATIONS, LABELS, LEAFLETS, MAGAZINES, PACKETS, PAMPHLETS, PROMOTIONAL MAILINGS, *AND MANY MORE.*

FEATURES WORK BY BASE DESIGN, BROWNS, BRUCE MAU DESIGN, CARTLIDGE LEVENE, CYAN, EGGERS + DIAPER, FABRICA, FARROW DESIGN, FRAME, FROST DESIGN, IDN, INTRO, IRMA BOOM, JOHNSON BANKS, KESSELSKRAMER, MADE THOUGHT, MARC NEWSON, MOTHER, NB: STUDIO, NORTH, PENTAGRAM, PHIL BAINES, SAGMEISTER INC., STATE, THE ATTIK, THE DESIGNERS REPUBLIC, THE KITCHEN, TOMATO, WHY NOT ASSOCIATES, WOLFF OLINS, UNA, *AND MANY OTHER INTERNATIONALLY RENOWNED DESIGNERS.*

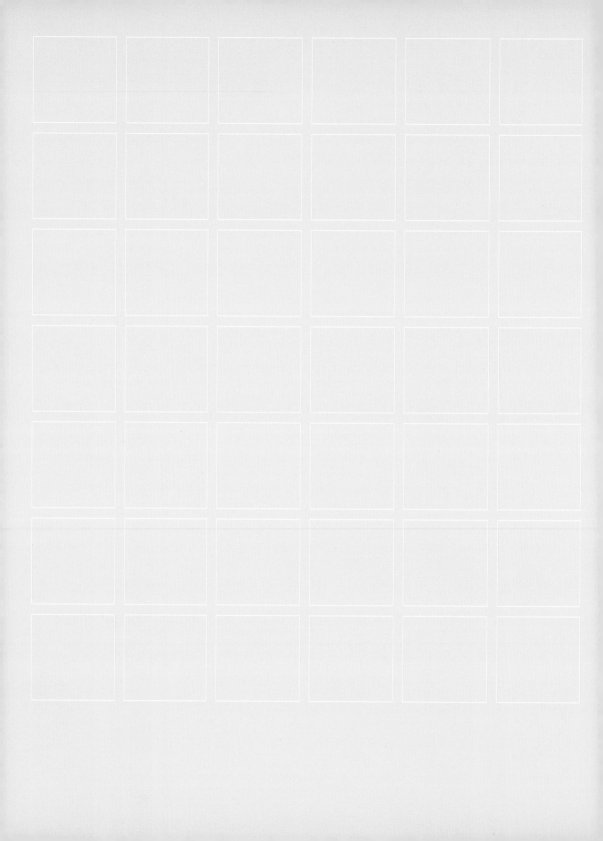

BOOKS AND MAGAZINES

010

DESIGNER: Irma Boom

PROJECT: *Gutenberg-Galaxie II*

DESCRIPTION: This chunky design monograph, on and by the Dutch designer Irma Boom, features a double-hinged cover, making it two books in one.

DESIGNER: Bohatsch Graphic Design

PROJECT: *Delugan_Meissl 2*

DESCRIPTION: Two separate case-bound books linked with a double-hinged cover. The clever binding allows both books to be read independently while enabling some spreads to work across both volumes.

011

012

DESIGNER: Intro

PROJECT: *The Colour of White*

DESCRIPTION: This book is contained within a substantial, white, cloth-covered slipcase, with the title of the project embossed on the surface.

DESIGNER: Project M Team

PROJECT: *Project M*

DESCRIPTION: This book of images is designed to reveal a secret message when the top corner of each page is folded into the spine.

014

DESIGNER: Blast

PROJECT: *Workout 2004*

DESCRIPTION: Section one of *Workout 2004* is a standard sadle-stitched booklet, bound into the outer-cover. Section two features loose-leaf pages bound into the outer cover with a thick rubber band.

DESIGNER: Base Design

PROJECT: *Women'secret look book*

DESCRIPTION: The loose pages of this fashion book are held together with just a rubber band.
This is kept in position by a notch that has been cut out of the top and bottom of each page.

015

016

DESIGNER: Julia Hasting

PROJECT: *Gordon Matta-Clark*

DESCRIPTION: This artist's monograph has a section cut out of its case-bound spine to reveal its construction. Brightly colored section threads have been used, giving the spine a greater beauty.

DESIGNER: Chicks on Speed

PROJECT: *It's a Project*

DESCRIPTION: This experimental book contains a variety of different sized pages. The erratically cut cover is just the start of the random cut-and-paste aesthetic of this book, which comes packaged in a cloth bag.

017

DESIGNER: David James Associates

PROJECT: *The Order of Things*

DESCRIPTION: This unique photographic book has no beginning or end, no title page or cover. The spine runs through the center of the book.

018

DESIGNER: Sagmeister Inc.

PROJECT: *Sagmeister*

DESCRIPTION: This book comes in a translucent, red, plastic slipcase, and the image on the front cover is of a calm Alsatian dog. However, once the slipcase is removed, the dog is transformed into a wild monster.

019

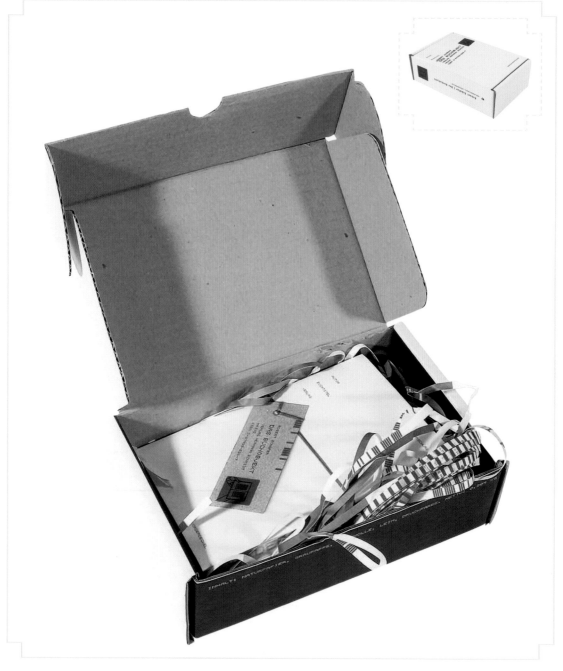

020

DESIGNER: Robert Schäfer

PROJECT: *Das Buchobjekt*

DESCRIPTION: This book comes packaged in a specially-made, white, corrugated cardboard box. Once the box is opened, the book is revealed cradled within a nest of shredded paper off-cuts.

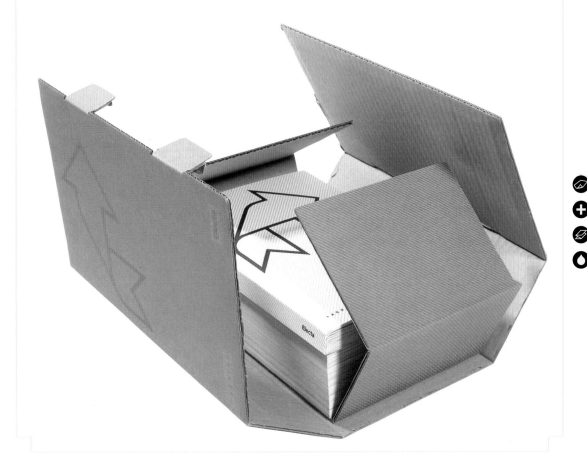

DESIGNER: Fabrica

PROJECT: *Mail Me*

DESCRIPTION: Two books beautifully contained within a custom-made, thick cardboard box.
The packaging offers more than just protection—it forms the true cover of the books within.

DESIGNER: Fabrica

PROJECT: *A Book About Food*

DESCRIPTION: This limited-edition book is packaged in a take-out tinfoil box. Fitting neatly inside, the result is a total package that instantly reflects the book's content.

DESIGNER: Hamish Muir

PROJECT: *The Phaidon Atlas of Contemporary Architecture*

DESCRIPTION: This huge architecture book, vast in both scale and weight, is contained within a specially-made, clear plastic case. The design of the case includes a handle to make the book easier to transport.

023

024

DESIGNER: State

PROJECT: *Motion Blur*

DESCRIPTION: This book and DVD of new media work are housed within a custom-built slipcase of black high-density foam. The title has been laser-cut into the foam to reveal fragments of the book's cover.

DESIGNER: Atelier Roger Pfund

PROJECT: *Hundert T Variationen*

DESCRIPTION: Reminiscent of an old cigar box, this highly unusual top-loading slipcase creates a striking and eclectic taster for the book itself, which features 100 different responses to the letter T.

025

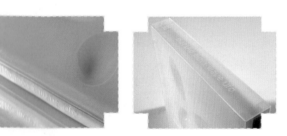

026

DESIGNER: Sagmeister Inc.

PROJECT: *Mariko Mori: Wave UFO*

DESCRIPTION: This book about the Japanese artist Mariko Mori, is enclosed in a white, translucent slipcase of polypropylene.

DESIGNER: Sagmeister Inc.

PROJECT: *Zumtobel Annual Report 01 02*

DESCRIPTION: The cover of this annual report for the lighting company Zumtobel features special plastic extrusions on both the front and back. The uncovered spine spells out the company's name.

027

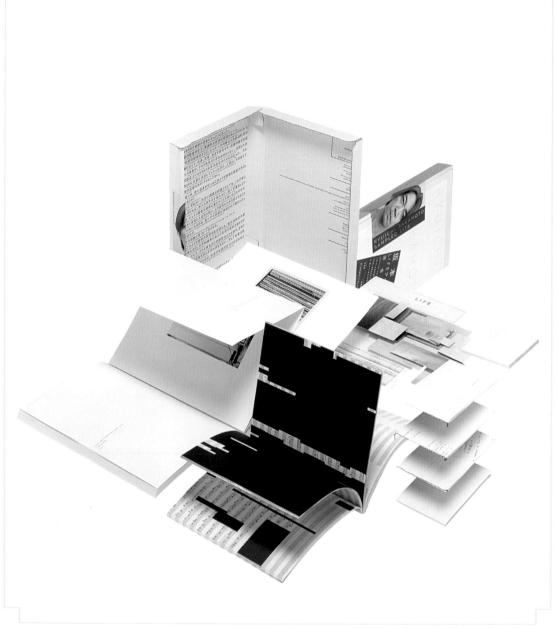

028

DESIGNER: Hideki Nakajima

PROJECT: *Ryuichi Sakamoto: Sampled Life*

DESCRIPTION: This package was produced to accompany composer Ryuichi Sakamoto's opera *Sampled Life*. It is comprised of four books and various loose-leaf elements housed within a special cardboard box.

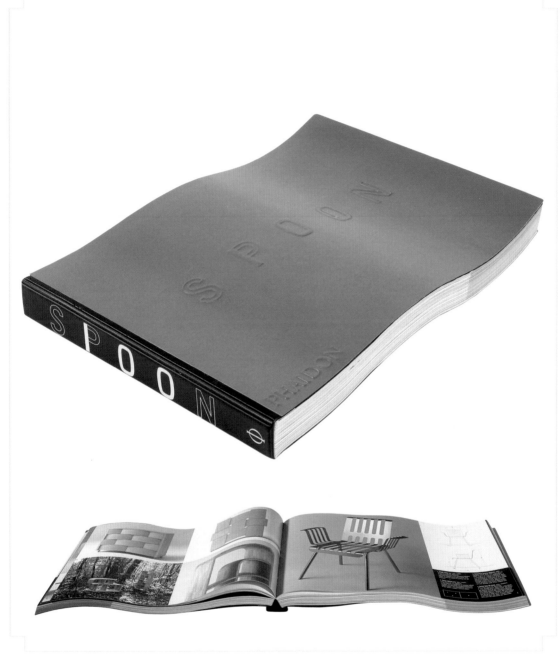

DESIGNER: Eggers + Diaper

PROJECT: *Spoon*

DESCRIPTION: This striking cover was created by stamping the title onto machine-bent sheets of metal. These sheets are bound to the book's endpapers causing the pages to follow the contours of the cover.

029

030

DESIGNER: Paula Scher at Pentagram

PROJECT: *Make it Bigger*

DESCRIPTION: Visually illustrating the title of this designer's monograph, the large-scale typography extends beyond the limits of the book's format. The type is printed off the cover and onto the edges.

DESIGNER: Helena Fruehauf

PROJECT: *Halfbreed 02*

DESCRIPTION: The cover of this self-initiated book project, features an embroidered, cloth-bound case that has been hand-stitched around the outside of the spine.

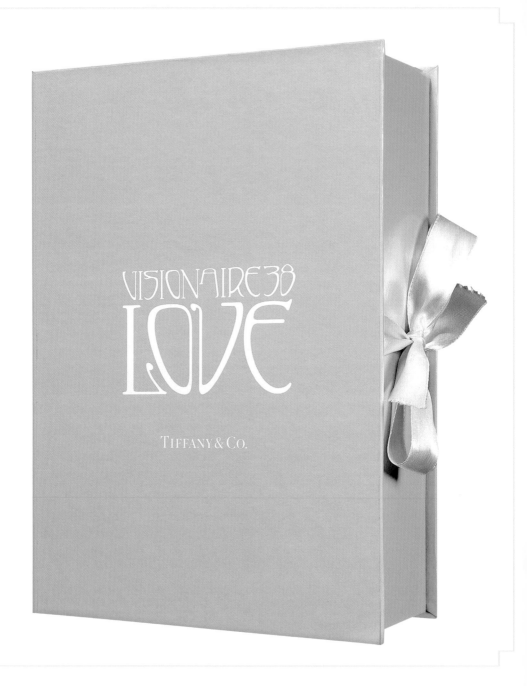

DESIGNER: Visionaire Magazine

PROJECT: *Love, Visionaire Issue No. 38*

DESCRIPTION: This unique issue of *Visionaire* magazine is packaged in a customized Tiffany box, which is tied with a white ribbon.

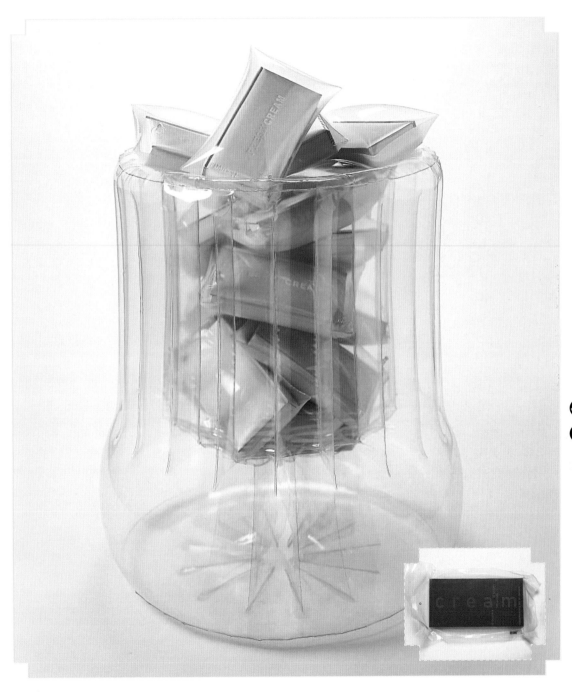

DESIGNER: Julia Hasting

PROJECT: *Cream* and *Fresh Cream*

DESCRIPTION: These two art books have been packaged in a way that suggests preservation of their fresh, contemporary content. *Cream* has been vacuum-packed, while *Fresh Cream* is packaged in a cushion of air.

033

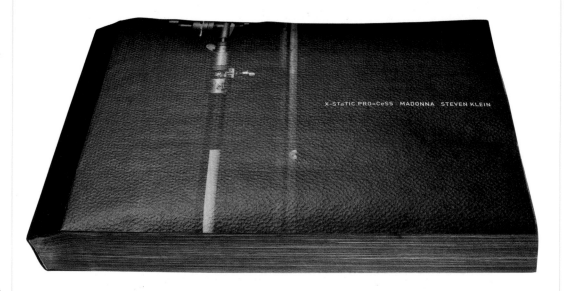

034

DESIGNER: Giovanni Bianco

PROJECT: *X-Static Pro=cess*

DESCRIPTION: This book was created to accompany an exhibition of photographs created by Steven Klein and Madonna. Both the paper and the printing process were developed especially for this unique book.

DESIGNER: Browns

PROJECT: *Pandora's Box*

DESCRIPTION: The production values for this book were extremely high. Pages are made from rubber, latex, leather, plastic, and transparent gels in response to the nature of the book's content.

035

036

DESIGNER: why not associates

PROJECT: *Guide to Ecstacity*

DESCRIPTION: The title of this book has been foil-stamped on the cover. The luggage tag around its middle conveys a sense of travel. Silk ribbons divide the pages.

DESIGNER: Sartoria, Mode 2, Harry Peccinotti, and Grafiche Damiam

PROJECT: *The Calendar*

DESCRIPTION: This calendar has a sense of luxury and sensuality. It has a hard cover of doubled cardboard and tissue overlay, blind-embossed with the title. The pages within are card with a high-gloss finish.

037

DESIGNER: Eggers + Diaper

PROJECT: *Witness*

DESCRIPTION: The cover of this book is made from aluminum with some circular, die-cut slits in the front. The slits reveal the surface of the CD.

DESIGNER: Carsten Nicolai, Olaf Bender, and Jonna Groendahl

PROJECT: *Auto Pilot: Carsten Nicolai*

DESCRIPTION: This book about the audio/visual artist Carsten Nicolai, includes a CD which is cleverly housed within the gate-fold. A die-cut circle reveals the central spine and a small circle of yellow.

040

DESIGNER: Raban Ruddigkeit

PROJECT: *Freistil*

DESCRIPTION: The bound edge of each section of this book makes full use of the exposed binding. The silver holographic cover boards, which refract the full spectrum of color, are referenced in the colors on the spine.

DESIGNER: Sans + Baum

PROJECT: *In Sight*

DESCRIPTION: Housed within a convenient hardback cover, this guide to design legibility for the visually impaired opens up to reveal two separate books.

041

042

DESIGNER: Made Thought

PROJECT: *Thinking Big: Concepts for Twenty-first Century British Sculpture*

DESCRIPTION: Two traditionally-bound books have been cleverly joined back-to-back to present two perspectives of a sculpture exhibition. The book comes inside a gray slipcase.

DESIGNER: The Attik

PROJECT: *(Noise) 3*

DESCRIPTION: The package of this self-published book by Attik consists of two sheets of metal which have been punched, molded, and formed to create a three-dimensional container.

044

DESIGNER: Stephen Gan, Greg Foley, and Judith Schuster

PROJECT: *Woman, Visionaire Issue No. 29*

DESCRIPTION: The outer packaging of this issue of *Visionaire* is constructed from injection-molded plastic in highly reflective silver. The book inside has a soft, blood-red flocked cover.

DESIGNER: Stephen Gan and Karl Lagerfeld

PROJECT: *The Emperor's New Clothes, Visionaire Issue No. 23*

DESCRIPTION: This issue of *Visionaire* is contained within a custom-built hinged wooden box with a leather carrying handle.

045

046

DESIGNER: Phil Baines

PROJECT: *Catalogue* and *Annette*

DESCRIPTION: This book comprises two separate publications, *Catalogue* and *Annette*, which are encased in a custom-made polystyrene box.

DESIGNER: John Crawford and Nick Thornton-Jones

PROJECT: *Ghost Menswear*

DESCRIPTION: Every page of this bulky book has been bonded to a sheet of 3mm board to create the illusion of a very solid, heavy block.

047

048

DESIGNER: Unica T

PROJECT: *o.T. book*

DESCRIPTION: The *o.T. book* was created by silk-screening abstract collages on to large sheets of rigid Perspex, which were then cut down to the final page size.

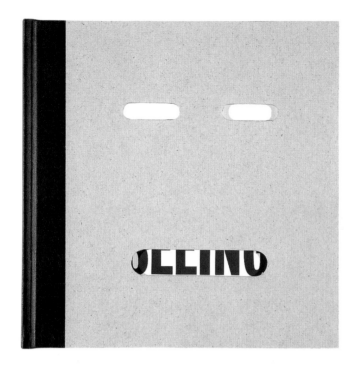

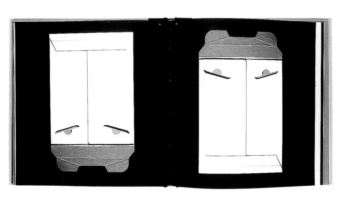

DESIGNER: Designframe

PROJECT: *Seeing: Doubletakes*

DESCRIPTION: This book cover is made of unprinted, plain gray bookbinding board out of which three holes have been die-cut to show a fragment of the title printed on the first page.

049

050

DESIGNER: North

PROJECT: Panache book

DESCRIPTION: Panache is a range of papers produced by McNaughton. The majority of pages in this book are blank, with the exception of sections showing examples of various production techniques.

DESIGNER: SAS

PROJECT: *BT: Charting the Virtual World*

DESCRIPTION: The last three-quarters of this book have a die-cut hole punched through all the pages, which reveals a CD held on the inside back cover.

051

052

DESIGNER: Paul Farrington

PROJECT: *Handbook for a Mobile Settlement*

DESCRIPTION: This book is formed by five sheets of A4 (8¹/₈ x 11⁵/₈ in) paper, printed both sides, then folded to A6 (4¹/₈ x 5³/₄ in). The sheets are bound with a white elastic band, resulting in a book with hidden pages.

DESIGNER: KesselsKramer

PROJECT: *ik ben Ben*

DESCRIPTION: This corporate manual for cellphone service provider Ben, has a specially-created cloth spine with the title of the book intricately sewn into it.

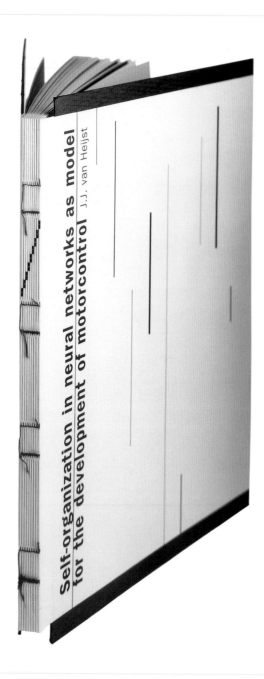

054

DESIGNER: Kristel Braunius

PROJECT: *Self-organization in neutral networks as model for the development of motorcontrol*

DESCRIPTION: By exposing the sewn sections' construction and through the use of bright red threads, the inner guts of this otherwise dry, academic book are exposed and turned into attractive features.

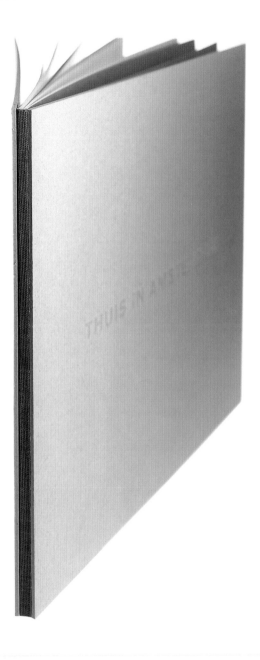

DESIGNER: KesselsKramer

PROJECT: *Thuis in Amsterdam*

DESCRIPTION: This book's title is embossed and foil-blocked with a clear varnish onto the pale turquoise cover boards. The book is produced as sewn sections, with an olive green binding cloth visible on the spine.

055

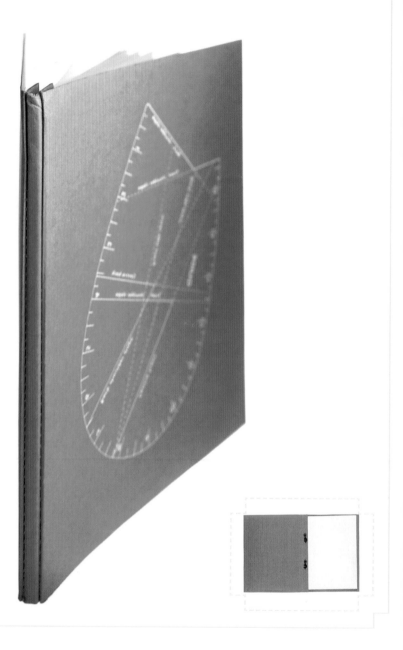

DESIGNER: John Cole

PROJECT: *Guidelines to the System*

DESCRIPTION: This artist's book has a cover made from manilla colored pattern-cutters board which has been doubled back on itself for added stability, and stitched together with white thread.

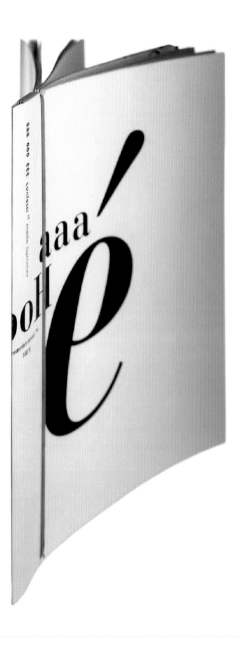

DESIGNER: Melle Hammer

PROJECT: *AAA OOO EEE – Confetti 25*

DESCRIPTION: The cover of this book is printed on a cast-coated stock in black and white, and bound with an elastic band.

057

058

DESIGNER: Britta Möller

PROJECT: *Kijken & Denken*

DESCRIPTION: Working as one main book and two smaller text books, this artist's monograph comes inside a numbered plastic bag. All three books are concertina-folded. The larger book has black Perspex covers.

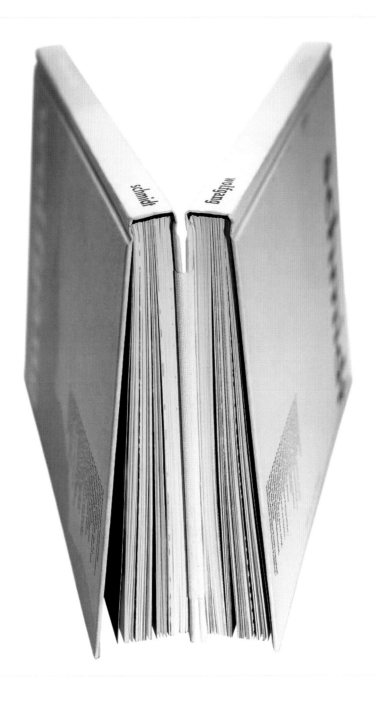

DESIGNER: Anke Jaaks

PROJECT: *Wolfgang Schmidt—Worte und Bilder*

DESCRIPTION: Produced as a thesis on the work of German graphic designer Wolfgang Schmidt, this unusually formatted book works across two separate case-bound volumes, themselves bound together.

059

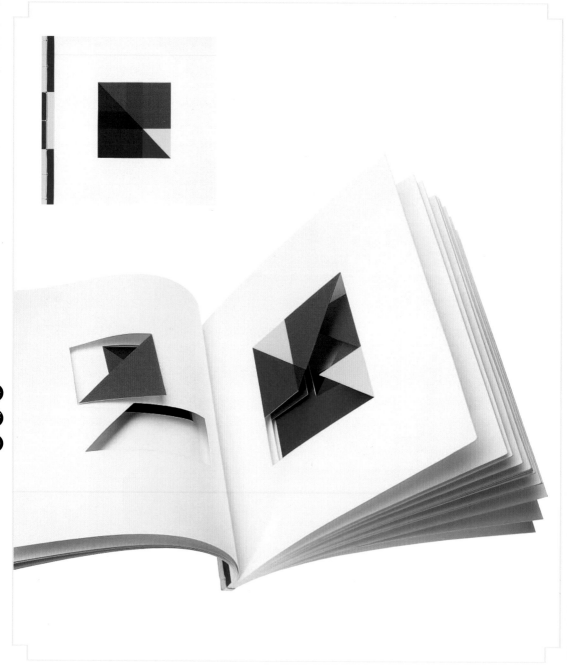

060

DESIGNER: Paolo Carraro

PROJECT: *The Impermanent*

DESCRIPTION: This limited-edition artist's book is silk-screen printed, cut, folded, and bound by hand. Each page is cut to reveal the pages beneath.

DESIGNER: Giorgio De Mitri, Patrizia Di Gioia, Nicola Peressoni, Francesco Forti, and Luca Bortolotti

PROJECT: *CUBE*

DESCRIPTION: *CUBE* is a limited-edition magazine. No expense is spared in its design and production, and no issue is the same. This issue was packaged in a black box and is designed to be like a small table.

061

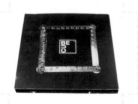

062

DESIGNER: Giorgio De Mitri, Patrizia Di Gioia, Nicola Peressoni, Francesco Forti, and Luca Bortolotti

PROJECT: *CUBE*

DESCRIPTION: This issue of *CUBE* magazine comes in an intricately die-cut card package that fits together like a puzzle.

DESIGNER: Giorgio De Mitri, Patrizia Di Gioia, Nicola Peressoni, Francesco Forti, and Luca Bortolotti

PROJECT: *CUBE*

DESCRIPTION: Sandwiched between two chunks of black foam, this issue of *CUBE* is presented as a three-dimensional cube. Once separated, the two pieces of foam act as a plinth on which to rest the book.

063

064

DESIGNER: Kevin Grady and Colin Metcalf

PROJECT: *GUM*

DESCRIPTION: Each issue of *GUM* magazine comes wrapped in its own specially-designed package, making them highly collectible items and giving them a gift-like feel.

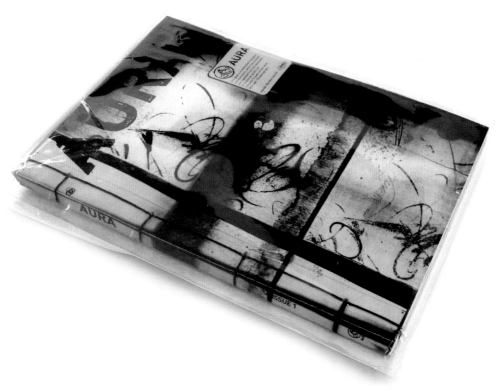

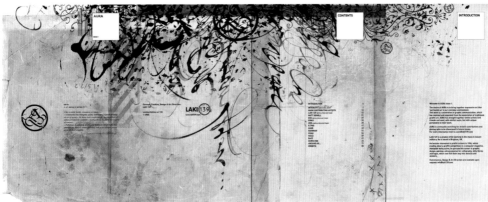

DESIGNER: LAKI 139

PROJECT: *AURA*

DESCRIPTION: Printed on a range of different stocks, this experimental magazine showcasing the work of 12 graffiti artists and illustrators has the feel of a sketchbook. The cover is coated in Yacht varnish.

065

066

DESIGNER: Amelia Gregory, Scott Bendall, and Asger Bruun

PROJECT: *Amelia's magazine*

DESCRIPTION: Issue 2 of this experimental magazine comes with a die-cut cover and a Tatty Devine pendant, which was nestled into the magazine by die-cutting a hole into the first 18 pages.

DESIGNER: Amelia Gregory

PROJECT: *Amelia's magazine*

DESCRIPTION: Issue 4 of *Amelia's magazine* was fully interactive, featuring a scratch-and-sniff cover and smelly pens customized with the *Amelia's magazine* logo. These can be used to color the illustrations within.

067

068

DESIGNER: Dave Eggers and Eli Horowitz

PROJECT: *McSweeney's*

DESCRIPTION: Issue 16 of this magazine, designed to look like a book, folds unexpectedly to reveal the magazine as well as some other items neatly contained within small pockets.

DESIGNER: Dave Eggers and Eli Horowitz

PROJECT: *McSweeney's*

DESCRIPTION: Issue 17 of *McSweeney's* magazine resembles a pile of junk mail. A number of accompanying items are bound together with a white rubber band.

070

DESIGNER: Luca Lonescu and Michelle Hendriks

PROJECT: *Refill*

DESCRIPTION: This issue of *Refill* magazine comes sealed in an industrial-type, black plastic bag.

DESIGNER: Markus Dreßen

PROJECT: *spector cut+paste*

DESCRIPTION: This issue of *spector cut+paste* magazine has a number of spot UV-varnished circles on the front cover. These are perforated and can be pushed out.

072

DESIGNER: Markus Dreßen

PROJECT: *spector cut+paste*

DESCRIPTION: The card cover of this issue is blank, except for an embossed pattern mimicking the metal exterior of a laptop. Open it, and there's the keyboard; open the next leaf, and there's a cut-out mouse.

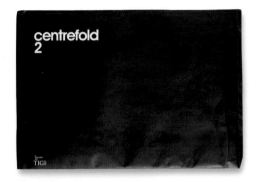

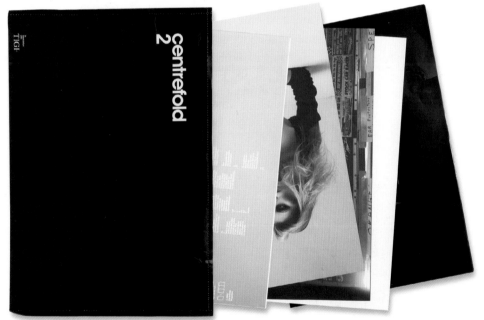

DESIGNER: BB/Saunders

PROJECT: *Centrefold*

DESCRIPTION: This magazine is made up of a series of interleaved pages—or posters—that feature the work of young image-making talent. It is large-format, unbound, and comes in a stitched and sealed bag.

073

074

DESIGNER: Ralf Herms

PROJECT: *+rosebud*

DESCRIPTION: This issue of *+rosebud* is more like a book than a magazine. The black, hardback cover is foil-blocked with the title and cover illustration, making for a magazine that is solid and luxurious.

DESIGNER: Mark Gainor

PROJECT: *Made*

DESCRIPTION: Inspired by vintage books, *Made* magazine has a real sense of quality. It is bound with a hardback cover, canvas spine, and silver foil-blocked Adobe Caslon Pro typeface.

075

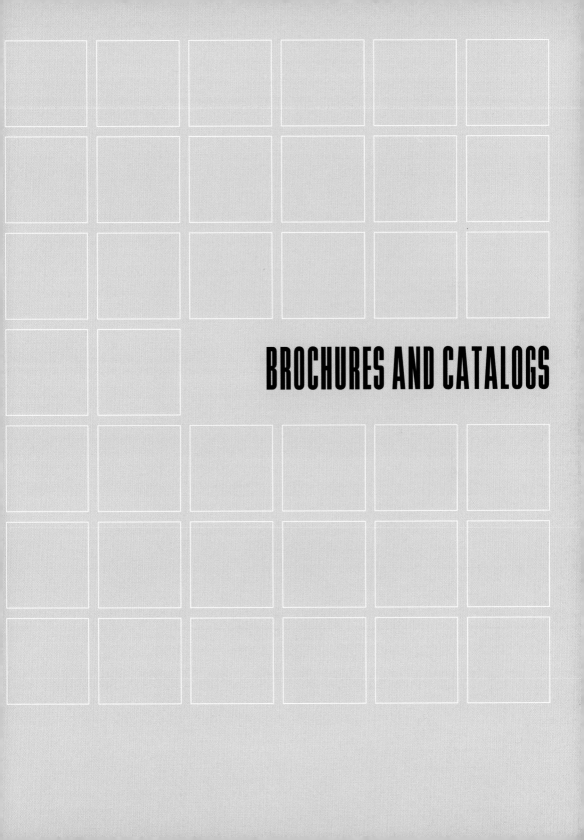

BROCHURES AND CATALOGS

078

DESIGNER: The Kitchen

PROJECT: *Levi's RED: Glass*

DESCRIPTION: This irregular-shaped fashion brochure box echoes the image of the shard of glass on its lid. The lid is removed to reveal nine individual sheets of board, all cut to the same irregular shape.

Anna Barriball
David Musgrave

Recognition Anna Barriball, Davi...

19 July – 21 September 2003
Monday to Saturday 10.00am –
Sunday until 9.00pm)
Admission free (Bank Holidays 12.00pm – 7.00pm)

DESIGNER: A2-Graphics/sw/hk

PROJECT: *Recognition*

DESCRIPTION: This artist's catalog for two separate shows is protected by two separate dust jackets folded horizontally so that, when wrapped around the book, the group title becomes legible.

079

080

DESIGNER: Cartlidge Levene

PROJECT: *9 Kean Street, Covent Garden*

DESCRIPTION: This lavish property brochure incorporates two books bound into one double-spined W cover, the centerfold of which is perforated allowing them to be separated.

DESIGNER: Eg.G

PROJECT: *Onitsuka Tiger*

DESCRIPTION: Contained within a purpose-made box, the two thin editions of this brochure are given a precious quality. Both collections are bound in the traditional Japanese manner, with red thread.

081

The National Centre for Business & Sustainability (NCBS) is a sustainable solutions organisation. This means that environmental protection and social responsibility are at the heart of the company's business activities.

We are committed to helping individuals and organisations minimise the environmental and social impacts of their activities. And because we believe in 'practising what we preach', we will endeavour to minimise those impacts arising from our own activities.

082

DESIGNER: Origin

PROJECT: Brochure for the National Centre for Business & Sustainability

DESCRIPTION: This brochure is made from 100 percent recycled, chlorine-free board. It features no ink and the type is debossed throughout.

DESIGNER: Roundel

PROJECT: Lanagraphic catalog

DESCRIPTION: This promotional brochure for Zanders Lanagraphic papers consists of two books attached by a single cover.

083

084

DESIGNER: Sunday-Vision

PROJECT: Orine catalog

DESCRIPTION: Intricate paper folding and decorative patterns are used here to create a catalog that has a kaleidoscope effect when it is opened and closed.

DESIGNER: Adjective Noun

PROJECT: *Fever*

DESCRIPTION: This highly-reflective souvenir brochure for Kylie Minogue's *Fever* tour, is packaged in a silver bubble-wrapped envelope, mimicking the futuristic feel of the show.

085

086

DESIGNER: NB: Studio

PROJECT: 40th Anniversary D&AD Awards brochure

DESCRIPTION: A foil and wax-based engraving technique called Dufex was used to give this brochure its unique quality. The corner has been die-cut at a 40 degree angle.

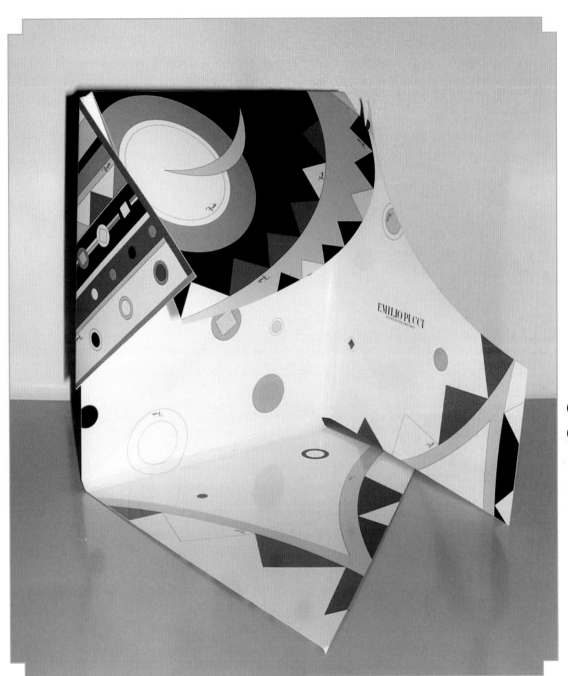

DESIGNER: Work in Progress

PROJECT: Pucci promotional catalog

DESCRIPTION: This catalog for the Pucci fashion house has been printed with one of Emilio Pucci's original 1960s patterns and then die-cut and folded in a way that makes it both original and unique.

087

DESIGNER: Sea Design

PROJECT: Catalog for Matthew Williamson fashion show

DESCRIPTION: The cover of this catalog is so reflective that you can clearly see your face in it and, as you move it, the color changes from gold to pink to blue to green.

DESIGNER: Spin

PROJECT: *Animals*

DESCRIPTION: This catalog has a small book within the main book. This mini book is printed on gray, uncoated stock in contrast to the main image section that is gloss.

090

DESIGNER: Mode

PROJECT: *Lostrobots*

DESCRIPTION: This limited-edition portfolio for a photographers' agent has a special foiled surface that seems to radiate heat and light as the color reacts to a light source.

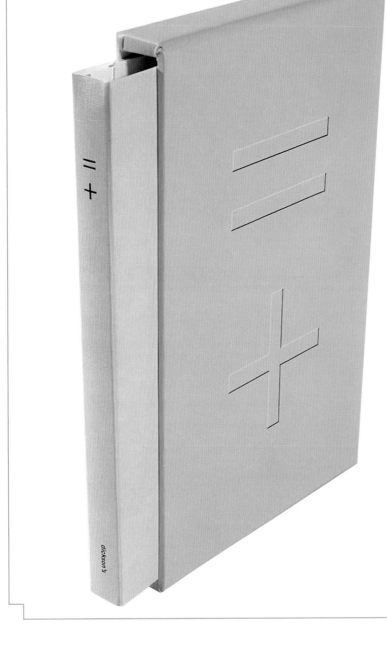

DESIGNER: Ph.D

PROJECT: *Dickson's: The Science of Sensation*

DESCRIPTION: Produced for Dickson's, a specialist printers, this brochure utilizes every unusual printing process in the company's vast arsenal.

DESIGNER: Projekttriangle

PROJECT: *Form+Farbe*

DESCRIPTION: The series of loose pages in this brochure are sandwiched between two pieces of board and held together by a thick rubber band.

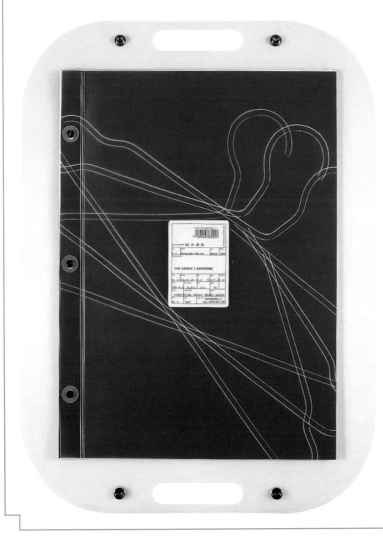

DESIGNER: Area

PROJECT: *One Woman's Wardrobe*

DESCRIPTION: The cover for this large-format exhibition catalog is made from polypropylene.
The back cover is enlarged to include the carrying handles and press-stud fastenings.

093

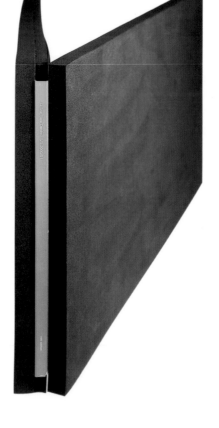

094

DESIGNER: Jaq La Fontaine

PROJECT: G-Star Raw Denim brochure

DESCRIPTION: This brochure comes packaged in a black, high-density foam box,
which is an integral part of the brochure cover.

DESIGNER: Olly.uk.com

PROJECT: Levi's Vintage Clothing brochure

DESCRIPTION: This book for Levi's vintage denim collection comes in its own distressed-denim dust jacket. Each cover went through a rigourous process of ageing and distressing.

095

096

DESIGNER: Mark Diaper

PROJECT: *The Missing Voice (Case Study B)*

DESCRIPTION: This is a beautifully produced catalog for an event organized by Artangle and the Whitechapel Gallery in London. The catalog contains an audio CD, which is held in place with a small

The Missing Voice (Case Study B) > > > > > > > >

foam button. It has a thin sheet of black sponge bound into the inside front and back covers. This gives it a very tactile feel and quality. It is singer-sewn, meaning a sewing machine has been used to bind all the pages together. The main image section of the catalog has been French folded, printing black-and-white images on the outside and color on the inside.

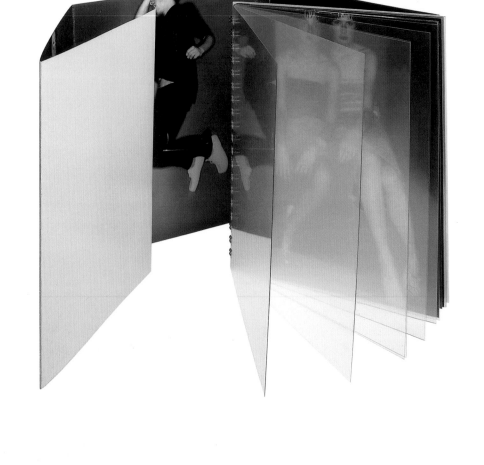

DESIGNER: Area

PROJECT: Paul & Joe Spring/Summer fashion catalog

DESCRIPTION: A mirror-like quality is created on the introductory pages of this catalog through the use of thin, clear sheets of acetate. As these are peeled away, the photography pages are revealed.

DESIGNER: Cartlidge Levene

PROJECT: *Designing Effective Annual Reports*

DESCRIPTION: This self-promotional brochure is concertina-folded and can be viewed as a conventional book or extended out to a length of over 12½ feet (3.8m).

099

DESIGNER: Herman Lelie

PROJECT: *Ophiuchus Collection*

DESCRIPTION: This exhibition catalog is produced as a concertina-folded book without a bound spine, allowing it to be stretched out into a long strip.

DESIGNER: Cartlidge Levene

PROJECT: Canal Building brochure

DESCRIPTION: The two sections of this brochure are separated by a gatefold, cover-weight page which wraps around the whole first section and ends on the inside front, neatly dividing the brochure.

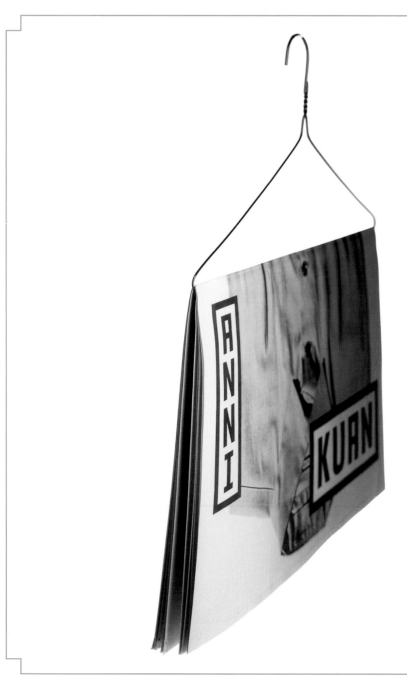

102

DESIGNER: Sagmeister Inc.

PROJECT: Anni Kuan Design brochure

DESCRIPTION: Produced on a modest budget, this fashion brochure was printed on newsprint by local newspaper printers. The brochure was then bound by simply hanging it from a wire coat hanger.

DESIGNER: Takaaki Matsumoto

PROJECT: *Material Dreams*

DESCRIPTION: The cover of this brochure is made from a heavily textured stock with the title embossed in the center. It is bound with rivets and finished with a delicate lace bow.

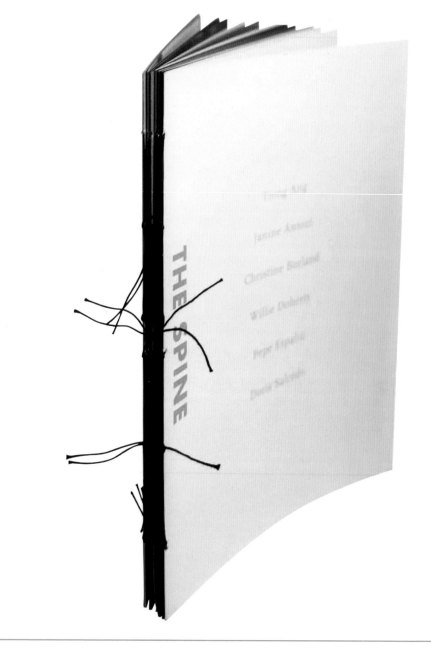

104

DESIGNER: Irma Boom

PROJECT: *The Spine | Da Appel*

DESCRIPTION: This artists' exhibition catalog uses the title of the show, *The Spine*, as its inspiration. Six eight-page booklets are neatly bound together with black thread, making a real feature of the spine.

DESIGNER: Wolff Olins

PROJECT: *Yacht – to the next curve*

DESCRIPTION: This special launch brochure for a rebranded company comes in the shape of a black cloth-covered, case-bound book. The company name, printed down the spine, bleeds around the edges.

105

DESIGNER: Cyan

PROJECT: *Form + Zweck 11/12*

DESCRIPTION: *Form + Zweck* is a design journal published in Germany. This issue comes as a sealed block with no obvious means of entry. On closer investigation, along one edge there is a discreet perforated

crease fold. With a certain degree of care, one can peel open the book to reveal the content.
Once inside, the reader is requested to complete the binding process following a set of instructions
printed on the back cover. A series of holes hold eight binding rivets which need to be removed and placed
in the vertical holes down the spine.

108

DESIGNER: Union Design

PROJECT: *The Tangerine Book*

DESCRIPTION: This brochure, bound using two screws, is two books in one. Each alternate page is cut ⅛ in (3mm) shorter. This means that different content is revealed depending on which way one flicks the book.

DESIGNER: KesselsKramer

PROJECT: Brochure for Hans Brinker Budget Hotel

DESCRIPTION: A hotel brochure that sells the "frightening" effects of spending a night in one of its rooms. The content is cut down the middle, allowing "before and after" case studies of various patrons of the hotel.

110

DESIGNER: Mark Diaper and Hans Bockting, UNA

PROJECT: Catalog for art exhibition

DESCRIPTION: The first section of this book was die-cut with a series of circles that were deliberately off-set to mimic the appearance of the larynx.

DESIGNER: Christie's International Media Division

PROJECT: Auction catalog

DESCRIPTION: The black matte jacket of this auction catalog is covered with hundreds of close but neatly spaced tiny holes, giving the catalog a very contemporary, industrial feel.

112

DESIGNER: Mother

PROJECT: Promotional brochure

DESCRIPTION: This self-promotional piece by Mother takes on a biblical theme. The box houses a promotional video, a brochure that looks like a bible, and a candle.

make sense of it all
a browns perspective
jonathan ellery
falmouth college of arts
main lecture theatre
friday 21st may
2.00pm 1999

atelierbrownscdtdesig
nhouseergofarrowgra
phicthoughtfacilityhg
vimaginationjannuzzi
smithkaye(tony)lambi
enairnmufnorthomnifi
cpentagramquay(davi
d)randsastomatounav
incefrostwolffolinsxya
mamotozigguratmake
senseofitall★◎➔✳!@?

screen printed by artomatic 0181 896 6666 paper supplied by fedrigoni 0541 555 517 printed on sirio

DESIGNER: Browns

PROJECT: Self-promotional brochure

DESCRIPTION: Browns chose this large-format, newspaper-style brochure as a way of promoting their work and ethos.

DESIGNER: KesselsKramer

PROJECT: Promotional brochure

DESCRIPTION: Joke-shop design from the Dutch pranksters. KesselsKramer created this pastiche of a typical joke beard packaging to promote their company.

114

DESIGNER: Delikatessen

PROJECT: Self-promotional item

DESCRIPTION: For this self-promotional mailing, an original Action Man doll was newly dressed and equipped with a small portfolio.

116

DESIGNER: NB: Studio

PROJECT: Self-promotional brochure

DESCRIPTION: NB: Studio produced this brochure in the form of a pack of cards. Each card features an image from a piece of work or project they had undertaken.

DESIGNER: Graça Abreu Design

PROJECT: *Book of Thoughts*

DESCRIPTION: This hardback promotional brochure mimics a luxury handmade diary. The leather-bound cover is tied together by a leather ribbon.

DESIGNER: Bruce Mau Design

PROJECT: Catalog for an art exhibition

DESCRIPTION: This catalog comes in the form of 50 loose-leaf posters in a white box. The box is blind-embossed on the front and on the spine.

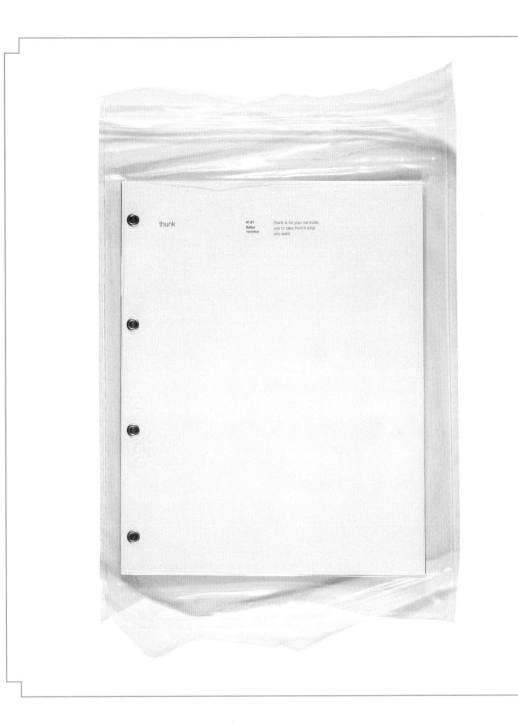

DESIGNER: Navy Blue

PROJECT: Self-promotional brochure

DESCRIPTION: This brochure is held together by four eyelets. It has then been vacuum-sealed giving it a firm and solid feeling.

119

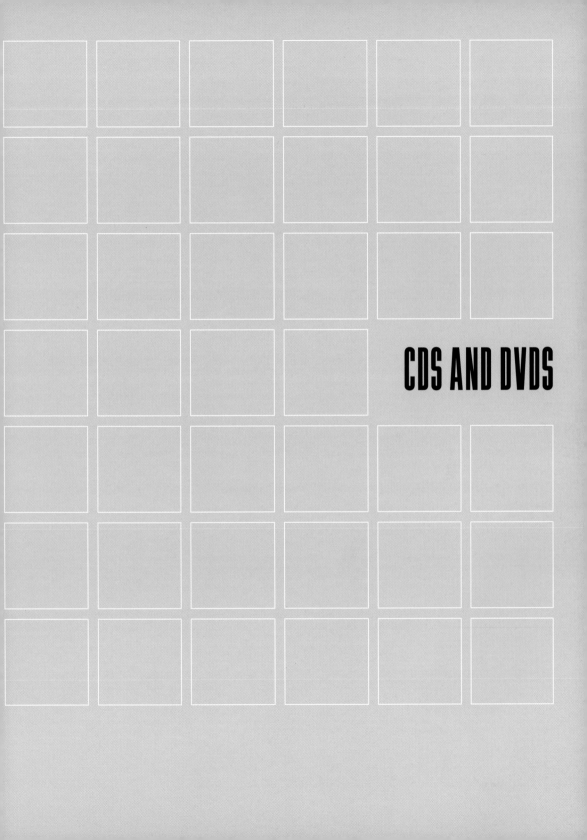

CDS AND DVDS

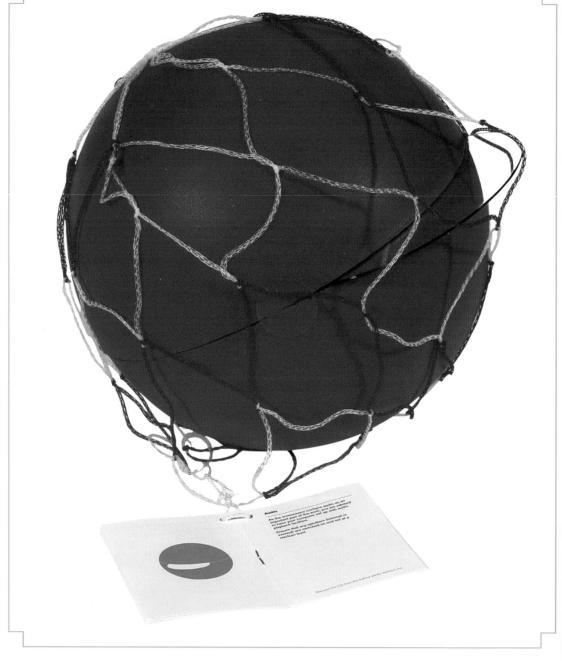

122

DESIGNER: Dowling Design

PROJECT: *Colour Match*

DESCRIPTION: This CD packaging and booklet for artist Simon Patterson is quite unique.
The high-density foam ball comes in a string net. The CD is concealed in a slot in the ball.

DESIGNER: Gunnar Thor Vilhjalmsson

PROJECT: Auxpan Elvar CD cover

DESCRIPTION: This CD cover is cardboard, on which a sticker, printed with a graphic, has been set. A hand-stitched, velcro strip fastens the case, and the whole thing comes in a soft silk-screen printed bag.

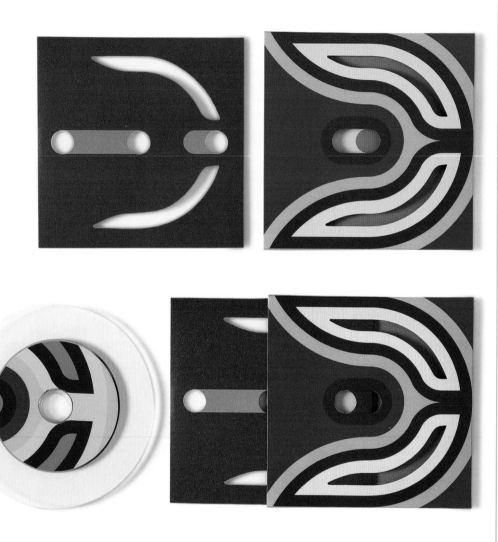

124

DESIGNER: Fred Deakin for Airside

PROJECT: *Spacewalk*, Lemon Jelly

DESCRIPTION: At first glance, this intricately die-cut CD sleeve appears empty, even when the inner wallet is removed. This is because the die-cut holes in the sleeve only show the transparent edge of the CD.

DANIEL
BEDINGFIELD
GOTTA
GET
THRU
THIS

ALBUM SAMPLER

DESIGNER: Michael Nash Associates

DESCRIPTION: *Gotta Get Thru This*, Daniel Bedingfield

DESCRIPTION: The bold type for the outer case of this CD cover has been brassplate die-cut to reveal the inner fluorescent orange sleeve.

125

126

DESIGNER: Jutojo

PROJECT: *In Between*, Jazzanova

DESCRIPTION: This chunky, book-like package is made up of six die-cut pieces of card. These have been cloth-bound and when closed present the viewer with a complete, unbroken image.

DESIGNER: WA75

PROJECT: Tom & Joy CD

DESCRIPTION: The closing flap of this CD case has been neatly die-cut in the profile of one of the artists. A belly band holds the Digipak closed and also contains the artists' names.

127

128

DESIGNER: Yacht Associates

PROJECT: *Electrastars*, TLM

DESCRIPTION: This unprinted disc sits inside a clear jewel case, that comes in a plain white, die-cut slipcase. Cyan, magenta, yellow, and black CDs were produced for this commercial release.

DESIGNER: Erik Torstensson for Winkreactive

PROJECT: *Swiss 1*, Various artists

DESCRIPTION: This packaging is modern and clean. Type was screen-printed on the white jewel case in white ink. The card slipcase has been embossed with the album's title.

129

130

DESIGNER: Farrow Design

PROJECT: *Let It Come Down*, Spiritualized

DESCRIPTION: This CD case features the image of a serene-looking girl molded into the plastic.
The track listing is embossed on the card inner sleeve.

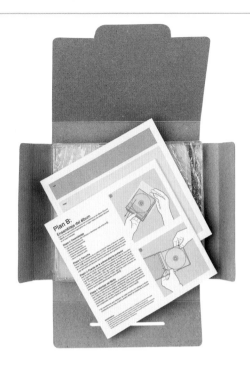

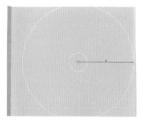

DESIGNER: Plan B

PROJECT: *Okoumé*

DESCRIPTION: Inside this brown box are the components necessary to build your own CD. Included in the pack is a shrink-wrapped jewel case, card inserts, stickers, and a full set of assembly instructions.

133

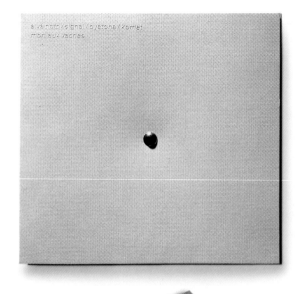

132

DESIGNER: Alorenz

PROJECT: *Alvo Noto, Signal, Byetone and Komet*, Various artists

DESCRIPTION: The type for this compilation CD has been blind-embossed onto pure white, textured 400gsm stock. The CD is held in a four-panel folded card cover by a paper binder.

DESIGNER: Salt for bombthedot

PROJECT: A series of albums by various electronic artists on the U-Cover label

DESCRIPTION: Each cover consists of a four-color printed, inner card sleeve featuring a different illustration or photograph, and a plain outer card sleeve that has the U-Cover logo die-cut into it.

134

DESIGNER: Silvio Waser at Buffer Für Gestaltung

PROJECT: *Part 1-14*, Solarium

DESCRIPTION: This CD is encased in a wooden box. The graphic elements were screen-printed in one color onto the box, while inside the disc sits on a mat to prevent it being damaged by the wood.

DESIGNER: Jeremy Plumb and Dan Poyner for Traffic

PROJECT: *Earthless*, Gintare

DESCRIPTION: No expense has been spared in the production of this lavish wood and steel CD case. The cover has been silk-screen printed with the title.

135

136

DESIGNER: Salt for bombthedot

PROJECT: *Ant-hology*, Various artists

DESCRIPTION: This limited-edition CD comes in a metal box that was laser-cut and bent to the required dimensions. Two regular Digipak CD trays hold the CDs.

DESIGNER: Chris Bilheimer

PROJECT: *Warning*, Green Day

DESCRIPTION: This green plastic cover with screen-printed images opens to reveal a 40-page book and CD housed in a cardboard folder.

138

DESIGNER: Peter and Paul

PROJECT: CD packaging for White Trash

DESCRIPTION: Peter and Paul hand made 30 of these covers for White Trash using a mix of materials they had lying around in their studio.

DESIGNER: MEEM

PROJECT: *MEEM*

DESCRIPTION: Plywood—stained and unstained—brown felt, Velcro, printed paper, an ink stamp, and a hot stamp were all used to make this limited-edition CD package.

139

DESIGNER: Époxy

PROJECT: CD packaging for Dubmatique

DESCRIPTION: This cover is made from coroplast, a plastic substrate that looks and functions like corrugated board but is translucent and impervious to water.

DESIGNER: Taylor Deupree for 12k

PROJECT: *.aiff*, Various artists

DESCRIPTION: Made from Mylar, this package is cut like an old floppy disc. The packaging has a minimalist, pure feel.

142

DESIGNER: Hut Recordings

PROJECT: *Black Market Music*, Placebo

DESCRIPTION: This package has a patented opening mechanism—by pulling on the tab, the package opens at opposite ends of the cover.

DESIGNER: Fred Deakin for Airside with Sam Burford at Transient

PROJECT: *Lost Horizons*, Lemon Jelly

DESCRIPTION: This album package uses a six-panel, hardboard folding cover, with a matte exterior and a gloss interior.

143

144

DESIGNER: Moussi Bucy

PROJECT: CD packaging for Bulbul

DESCRIPTION: This heavy, solid, iron cover with bolt fastenings is in stark contrast to the colorful imagery on the disc. The type is metal-stamped onto the cover.

DESIGNER: Oliver Walker Gellender and Artomatic

PROJECT: *10*, various artists

DESCRIPTION: These clear discs are cut-and-polished, 10mm-thick sheet acrylic. They are attached by a thread and screw. The CDs were screen-printed matte black onto a black polycarbon disk.

146

DESIGNER: Alorenz

PROJECT: *Mort Aux Vaches*, Ryoji Ikeda

DESCRIPTION: This polypropylene, folded CD case is held together by a small plastic button. The type was screen-printed onto the outer cover.

CITY ROCKERS PRESENT FUTURISM 2.

Article 2. Section 1 (a).
Redressing the balance, claiming back from the past and the future the incentive in its purist form Musically a progression from its original, microcosmic enclave (futurism one, section 1a) it can be comparable to that split second of tranquillity before everything goes off. The 808 snare snap snapping faster and faster, with a Synth enthused Der Da Da Da Da reverberating around your eardrums, the hair standing up on the back of your neck as you catch your reflection a thousand times over in the glitter-ball. Wrestled away from the sweaty palms of the navel gazing minority it's swallow diving on the dance floor. It's Aggit-pop thrust back into the hands of the rightful multitude (See Appendix section 3, Cityrocks5CD)

FUTURISM.

 Silver Screen-Shower Scene
...tius, Sunglasses At Night
La Velvet), La La Land 5.Tck
...Gonna Die (Martini Brothers
...le, Fantasize 7.S.K. Da Da
Article 1 Section 1 (a).
A state wherein 2 or more similarly attired individuals dedicated to shifting identities and the challenge of modernistic aesthetic values, form revolutionary inspired groups with assumed various social/political objectives Aided by repetitive vibrations of an Electro/synthetic button pushing nature (something of a bleep bleep bleep generally orchestrated from Roland 808 Synth boxes drum machines and the like) it represents a radical departure from the previous regulatory movements incorporating many of the additional elements adopted from non-electronically enthused instrumentation Epoch reflective, its discotheque reverberations adds backbone to the cause against the prohibitive notions so prevalent in more sanitised expressionistic formulas (See Appendix section 2).

DESIGNER: David Smith for Milk

PROJECT: *Futurism 1* and *Futurism 2*, Various artists

DESCRIPTION: These solid-colored jewel cases come in clear slipcases, screen-printed with white typography. There is no photography or illustration.

148

DESIGNER: Fehler

PROJECT: *Gigue, Live @ A-Musik* (top), *The Pride of the South Side, Live @* WHPK (bottom), Stephen Mathieu and Warm Desk

DESCRIPTION: These CDs were printed on both sides and enclosed in flexible, transparent plastic C-Shell cases.

DESIGNER: Salt

PROJECT: *Episodes*, Vromb

DESCRIPTION: The tin for this limited-edition release is made from aluminum, which has been laser-cut and bent into shape. The band's logo has been screen-printed with a black-gloss ink on the lid.

149

150

DESIGNER: Chris Bilheimer

PROJECT: *New Adventures in Hi-Fi*, REM

DESCRIPTION: Inspired by an old photo of an elevator, the die-cut diamond shape in this slipcase matches the elevator window. The book cover is die-cut to match the elevator car.

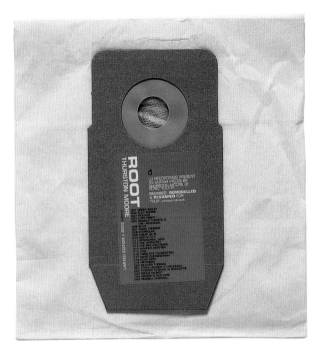

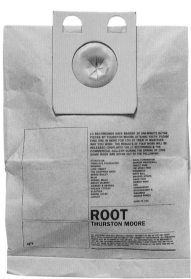

DESIGNER: Jon Forss for Non-Format

PROJECT: *Root*, compilation by Thurston Moore

DESCRIPTION: This CD comes packaged in a selection of screen-printed vacuum cleaner bags. The bags were stuffed with Kapok to suggest dust. The disc itself carries a color photograph of dust.

152

DESIGNER: 2GD

PROJECT: *Selvsving*, Oliver Zahle, Jens Korse, and Lars le Dous

DESCRIPTION: This 100 percent recycled-paper packaging is designed to look like a radio set.
When closed, die-cuts in the cover allow the consumer to use one of the discs like a radio tuning dial.

DESIGNER: Salt for bombthedot

PROJECT: *A Giant Alien Force*, Venetian Snares

DESCRIPTION: This CD comes packaged in a box with a 1970s-style image viewer.
The images on the viewer provide a visual accompaniment to the music on the disc.

153

154

DESIGNER: Michael Stipe of REM and Chris Bilheimer

PROJECT: *Up*, REM

DESCRIPTION: REM's *Up* album cover takes its inspiration from the corrugated packaging of a box of cookies, with its diamond-patterned design.

DESIGNER: Peter Maybury

PROJECT: *Dreaming Out Loudest*, Hard Sleeper

DESCRIPTION: A 72-page booklet accompanies this CD, which is packaged in a card box. The box is printed with pillow feathers and comes with a mini satin pillow enclosed.

156

DESIGNER: Elisabeth Kopf and the Vienna Art Orchestra

PROJECT: *Little Orchestra*, Vienna Art Orchestra

DESCRIPTION: This Plexiglas CD packaging is also a music box. Through some clever engineering and placement of holes, musical notes are played as the box is opened.

DESIGNER: Christof Steinmann

PROJECT: *Spezialmaterial Box*, Various artists

DESCRIPTION: This wooden box contains seven CDs and a booklet. It is made from MDF and the CDs are housed in simple jewel cases with self-adhesive CD labels.

157

158

DESIGNER: BMG

PROJECT: *See This Through and Leave*, The Cooper Temple Clause

DESCRIPTION: The CD is housed in a specially-produced, gold foil-blocked photograph album, which is foam-padded front and back and sealed by mock leather plastic.

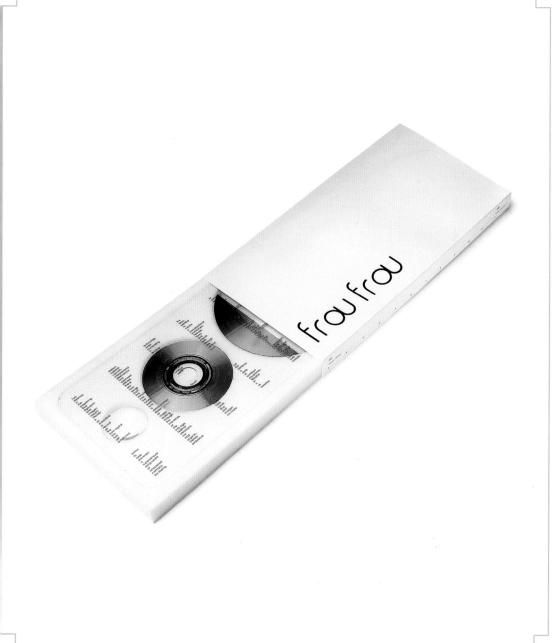

DESIGNER: Michael Nash Associates

PROJECT: *Breathe In* and *Details*, Frou Frou

DESCRIPTION: Beneath this PVC slipcase are two sheets. One of these is blank with the instructions "breathe on" in the corner. Warm breath makes lyrics written in heat-sensitive ink visible.

160

DESIGNER: Marc Newson

PROJECT: Torus CD case

DESCRIPTION: The Torus case was designed by Marc Newson to create a new form of CD packaging. The circular injection-molded lid and base has a screw mechanism to allow access to the disc.

DESIGNER: zoviet*france

PROJECT: *Popular Soviet Songs and Youth Music*, zoviet*france

DESCRIPTION: This CD is sandwiched between a number of different discs, including blank CDs dressed with printed flock and discs of gray felt cut from Red Army surplus caps.

DISK PERMIT MUST BE CLEARLY VISIBLE AT ALL TIMES

C879 UCH

DESIGNER: bhatoptics

PROJECT: *LMW*, Quinoline Yellow

DESCRIPTION: This whole album package is based on the theme of motoring, and uses a tax disc holder to house the CD.

DESIGNER: Antoine+Manuel

PROJECT: DVD packaging for Bootleg

DESCRIPTION: These DVD packages are constructed from thick Perspex and silk-screen printed with Helvetica Neue type. The slipcases have then been hot-stamped, giving them a very luxurious quality.

164

DESIGNER: Nike, Neverstop, and C505

PROJECT: *Nike Presto, Spirit of the Movement*

DESCRIPTION: This DVD packaging has been created using egg carton material.
It is completed with the inclusion of printed eggs on the disc.

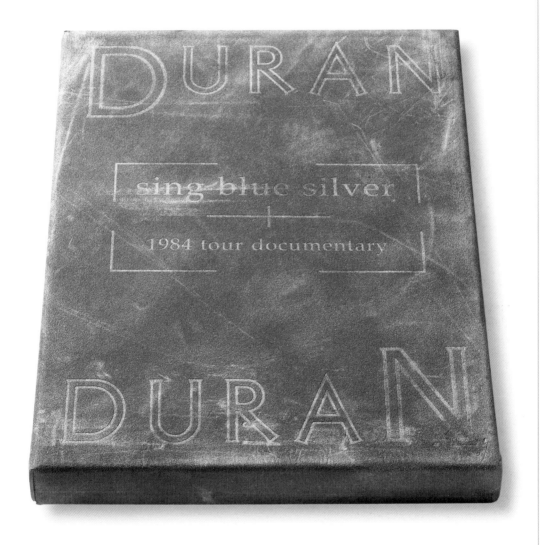

DESIGNER: The Red Room at EMI

PROJECT: *Duran Duran: Sing Blue Silver*, Duran Duran

DESCRIPTION: A fantastic blue velour material was selected to cover this basic clamshell DVD Digibox to make it something special. The cover has been embossed with the band's name and the DVD title.

165

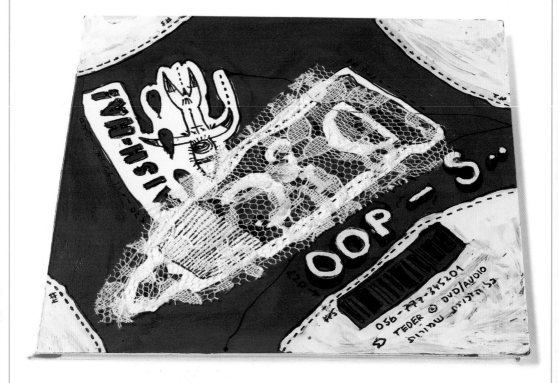

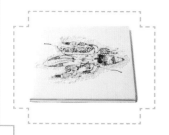

DESIGNER: Jewboy Corporation

PROJECT: DVD for Gal Tushia

DESCRIPTION: The design of this DVD packaging combines many arts and crafts methods with the use of several materials, including card and lace.

DESIGNER: Non-Format

PROJECT: *Stærk*, Various artists

DESCRIPTION: This custom-made DVD wallet has a tear strip that, once removed, reveals the title and the actual wallet beneath.

168

DESIGNER: Paramount

PROJECT: *Star Trek: The Original Series*

DESCRIPTION: Each of these plastic, molded DVD packages contains eight discs. The outer cases are made from hard plastic and clip shut at the top. They feature raised titles and the *Star Trek* logo.

DESIGNER: Form

PROJECT: *The Water Margin: Complete Series*

DESCRIPTION: This card slipbox houses 13 DVDs. The images on the spines of each disc have been designed to join up when they are in the correct order.

For YOUR EMMY
CONSIDERATION

FOX

170

DESIGNER: Erbe Design

PROJECT: Fox Emmy DVD mailing project

DESCRIPTION: This sophisticated set of commemorative DVDs comes packaged in a card slipcase. The covers are made from a heavy duty card, rather than plastic, giving them a sophisticated and stylish feel.

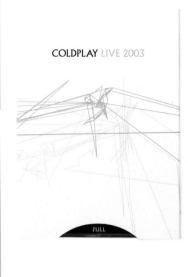

DESIGNER: Mark Tappin at Blue Source

PROJECT: *Coldplay Live 2003*

DESCRIPTION: This pull-out DVD format is a simple yet effective piece of engineering.
When the semicircular area on the edge of the cover is pulled, two DVD trays appear.

171

DESIGNER: Jennifer Garcia

PROJECT: *Elvis: Aloha from Hawaii*

DESCRIPTION: This DVD packaging has been gold foil-blocked and has stars added to the updated Elvis logo type. It has a great classic yet very contemporary feel.

DESIGNER: Kevin Reagan and Beck

PROJECT: *Guero*, Beck

DESCRIPTION: The cover package of this DVD takes the form of a hardback book. The simple, pure white cover is kept clean and minimal with the album title being applied in an off-white varnish.

173

174

DESIGNER: Tony Hung at Adjective Noun

PROJECT: *Fever 2002*

DESCRIPTION: This limited-edition DVD documents a concert on Kylie Minogue's Fever tour. It comes in a high-shine slipcase, mimicking the futuristic feel of the show.

DESIGNER: Matt Pyke at The Designers Republic

PROJECT: *Volatile Media*

DESCRIPTION: This DVD for a digital arts festival comes in a six-panel Digipak. The graphics are inspired by TV test cards, optical illusions, technical glitches, and the color clash of TV screens.

175

DESIGNER: Brett Kashmere

PROJECT: *Industry: Recent Works by Richard Kerr*, Richard Kerr

DESCRIPTION: This heavily textured packaging is really unusual in that the three variations of the DVD have individually handcrafted and painted covers.

176

DESIGNER: Point Blank Inc.

PROJECT: *The Hitchcock Collection*

DESCRIPTION: This collection of Alfred Hitchcock movies has been updated and neatly packaged in a card slipcase to give it a contemporary feel.

177

178

DESIGNER: Seb Jarnot

PROJECT: *Laurent Garnier: Unreasonable Live*

DESCRIPTION: This DVD is packaged in a standard jewel case, and comes with a limited-edition 12-inch single, both of which are housed in an outer box.

DESIGNER: Fry-Guy, Jaga Jankowska, and Guy Grember

PROJECT: *designFLUX*

DESCRIPTION: A slim, transparent DVD package has been used for this video magazine, enabling people to see the DVD and booklet inside.

179

180

DESIGNER: Jeff Jank

PROJECT: *Stones Throw 101*

DESCRIPTION: The package for this DVD was designed to look like an old library book. The cover features a textured print to give it the feel of an old leather-bound book.

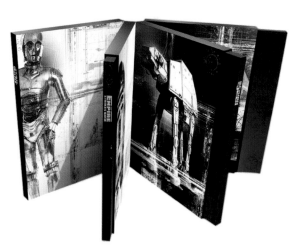

DESIGNER: Neuron Syndicate Inc.

PROJECT: *Star Wars* trilogy

DESCRIPTION: The packaging of this four-disc set is both concealing and revealing. With each slipcase or turn of the page, something new is uncovered.

181

DESIGNER: The Designers Republic

PROJECT: *WarpVision: The Videos 1989–2004*

DESCRIPTION: This DVD cover is styled like a hardback book, providing a real sense of weight and quality
The title is foil-blocked on the front.

DESIGNER: Animal Rummy

PROJECT: *Under Blackpool Lights*, The White Stripes

DESCRIPTION: This package for The White Stripes was produced with three different colored cases—black, white, and red. Each color case uses different transparencies as inserts within the DVD booklet.

183

184

DESIGNER: Dirk Rudolph

PROJECT: *In Extremo*

DESCRIPTION: Housed inside this luxurious outer box is a 10-panel Digipak and pullout poster. All have a matte-varnish finish printed with a Pantone metallic gold background.

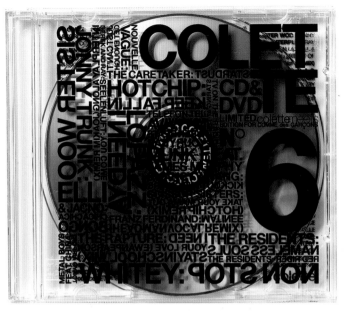

DESIGNER: Work in Progress

PROJECT: *Colette No 6*

DESCRIPTION: Maximizing the minimalist effect of the transparent jewel case, typography has been screen-printed in a single color directly on to the outer cases of these DVDs.

185

186

DESIGNER: Gabor Palotai

PROJECT: *Gabor Palotai: Maximizing the Audience: The Animated Book*

DESCRIPTION: The idea behind this DVD packaging was to make something very simple and controlled, using only a black-and-white color palette and with no imagery.

DESIGNER: Matt Maitland at Big Active

PROJECT: *The Last Minute*

DESCRIPTION: This DVD comes packaged in a translucent silver bag.

187

DESIGNER: Yoshi Sodeoka and Jason Mohr

PROJECT: *40 40 31*

DESCRIPTION: This is a limited-edition, handmade experimental art DVD. The transparent nature of the package, with only text on the cover, gives it a sense of simplicity.

DESIGNER: IdN

PROJECT: *Flips*

DESCRIPTION: *Flips* is a magazine/book that comes complete with a specially-made DVD.
The books act as packaging for the DVDs.

190

DESIGNER: IdN

PROJECT: *Tekko 03: Future Beautiful*

DESCRIPTION: This exhibition catalog has a book-style cover in a bright green, gloss finish, and comprises a deck of illustrated postcards and an accompanying DVD.

DESIGNER: Sartoria Comunicazione

PROJECT: *Defumo*

DESCRIPTION: The *Defumo* project included not only a DVD, but also a series of three limited-edition T-shirts. The cardboard package folds into four areas containing the T-shirts and the DVD.

191

GREETINGS, INVITATIONS, AND MAILERS

194

DESIGNER: Hornall Anderson Design Works

PROJECT: GGLO Architects invitation

DESCRIPTION: This matchbook-style invitation uses a series of deep, bright reds on a selection of vellum inserts. Each insert contains a printed image of a match or lit candles.

DESIGNER: Pylon

PROJECT: Festive mailing

DESCRIPTION: This playful Christmas mailout comes in the form of a miniature plastic traffic cone. It carries a sticker with a witty message from the designers.

196

DESIGNER: Thought Communications Ltd.

PROJECT: Festive greetings card

DESCRIPTION: This card has four perforated circles that push out to become drink coasters. Each carries its own promotional message.

DESIGNER: Perceptor

PROJECT: Festive mailing

DESCRIPTION: This fun promotional mailout is a "snowperson kit." Five pieces of coal and one carrot have been vacuum-sealed in a protective, inflated transparent bag.

FRÜHLINGS
GEFÜHLE

*

Inhalt zum Verzehr geeignet *

ANWENDUNG
Kurz vor Betreten
des Frühlingsfestes auf der
Zunge zergehen lassen.

WIRKUNGSWEISE
Frühlingsgefühle stellen
sich unmittelbar bei Verzehr ein.

NEBENWIRKUNGEN
Prickeln in Mund- und
Bauchbereich,
angenehmes Herzflattern,
in einigen Fällen
auch Lachfältchen.

a+o

198

DESIGNER: Factor Design

PROJECT: Party invitation

DESCRIPTION: The plastic container attached to this card invite contains "springtime beads," which create appropriately seasonal feelings when ingested. These were to be swallowed before entering the party.

DESIGNER: SEA

PROJECT: Invitation for the British Design & Art Direction Annual Show

DESCRIPTION: The invitation is set in a cardboard slipcase with screen-printed, malleable plastic rolled inside. The plastic unravels and reveals explanations of elements of the event.

200

DESIGNER: NB: Studio

PROJECT: D&AD invitation

DESCRIPTION: The cryptic message on this invitation can only be read when it is reflected in the mirror-board panel.

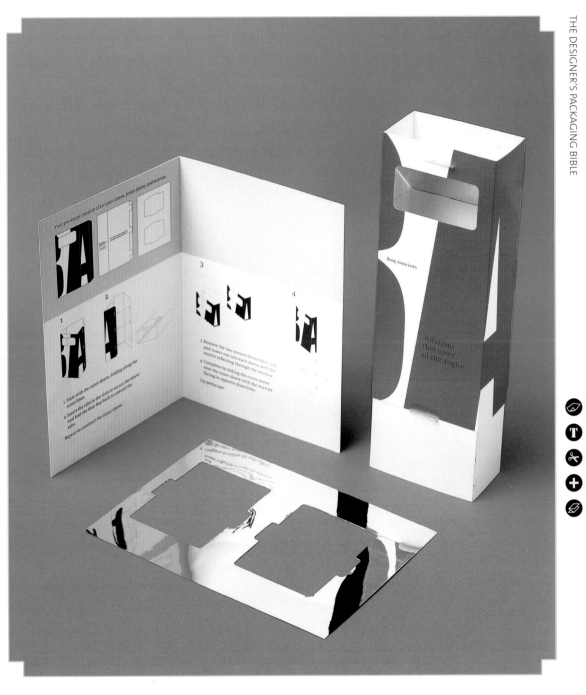

DESIGNER: Corina Fletcher and Boag Associates

PROJECT: Self-promotional mailout

DESCRIPTION: This self-promotional card can be assembled into a working periscope.
It comes with a set of step-by-step assembly instructions.

201

202

DESIGNER: Diesel Design

PROJECT: Promotional calendar

DESCRIPTION: This promotional calendar, sent out to Diesel Design's clients, comes as a series of card discs neatly packaged in a metal box. A magnetic clip holds the relevant disc to the top of the tin.

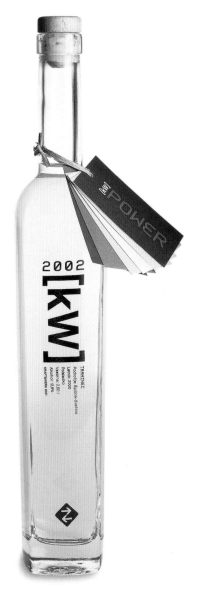

DESIGNER: Kraft & Werk

PROJECT: Promotional festive mailing

DESCRIPTION: Kraft & Werk had bottles of wine branded with their own logo to send out to their clients and friends as a promotional gift. The wine came packaged in a stylish card tube.

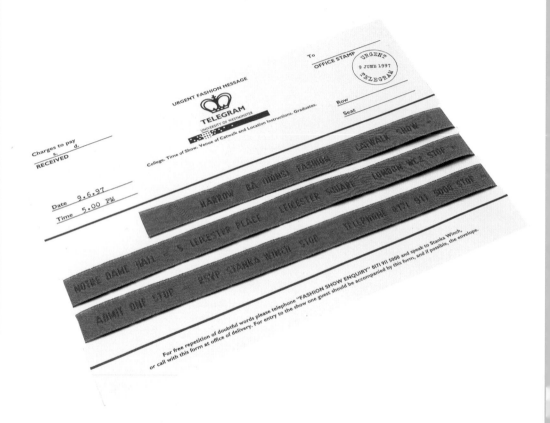

DESIGNER: Maxine Law

PROJECT: University of Westminster BA Fashion catwalk show invitation

DESCRIPTION: Maxine Law used the old-fashioned medium of a telegram card for this invitation. The ribbons were produced by a manufacturer specializing in creating woven labels for garments.

EINLADUNG

ANLÄBLICH MEINES 60.GEBURTSTAGES LADE
ICH EIN ZU EINEM PICKNICK MIT DEM
STREICHQUARTETT DER MECKLENBURGISCHEN
STAATSKAPELLE IM FRANKENHORST 7
AM ZIEGELSEE IN SCHWERIN

Wer der Einladung folgen möchte, finde sich
am 9.8.1997 um 10.45 Uhr an der Anlegebrücke der
Weißen Flotte gegenüber dem Schweriner Schloß ein

DESIGNER: Eggers + Diaper

PROJECT: Invitation for fund-raising picnic event

DESCRIPTION: The details of this event were printed on the napkin ring wrapped around a napkin.
The witty use of an unusual object makes the invitation engaging and memorable.

205

206

DESIGNER: Stocks Taylor Benson

PROJECT: Festive greetings card

DESCRIPTION: This humorous greetings card has an "emergency" Christmas tree lightbulb neatly encased in a red card box.

DESIGNER: Stocks Taylor Benson

PROJECT: Festive mailing

DESCRIPTION: This party popper has been modifed with streamers containing the names of the staff at Stocks Taylor Benson. It has then been packaged in a transparent plastic case, as if frozen in action.

208

DESIGNER: SEA

PROJECT: Rankin/GF Smith event invitation

DESCRIPTION: This invitation consists of a plastic wrap covering a camera-shaped box.
The paper printed inside shows shots by the photographer Rankin.

DESIGNER: David Hillman at Pentagram

PROJECT: Party invitation

DESCRIPTION: Pentagram designed this invitation as a pastiche of a 1960s seven-inch record. Details of the event were printed on each side of the label.

210

DESIGNER: Virgin Projects

PROJECT: Festive mailing

DESCRIPTION: Traditionally gift-wrapped T-shirts were sent out to Virgin's clients as a thank you for their interest and business over the year. The idea was to congratulate them by saying that they were stars!

DESIGNER: Max and Co

PROJECT: Promotional mailing

DESCRIPTION: The "Identity Protection Kit" cleverly combines the concepts of corporate and personal identity, comprising a novelty nose and glasses set, mounted inside a specially-commissioned box.

212

DESIGNER: Boxer Design

PROJECT: Birthday party invitation for Maya Polsky

DESCRIPTION: Enclosed in a gold corrugated cube box is a simple, letterpress card, a gold cord, and lots of feathers. When the card is pulled out of the box, the cord reveals a long feather boa.

DESIGNER: The Farm

PROJECT: Invitation to magazine launch party

DESCRIPTION: A delicate handmade box is the format for this invitation. Inside the box, a white script on a transparent film is revealed, under which lies a black feather, which is the recipient's passport to the venue.

214

DESIGNER: Plus One Design

PROJECT: Christmas greetings card

DESCRIPTION: This textile snowball was made to be hung on Plus One Design's office Christmas tree. It comes packaged in a silver box tied shut with blue ribbon.

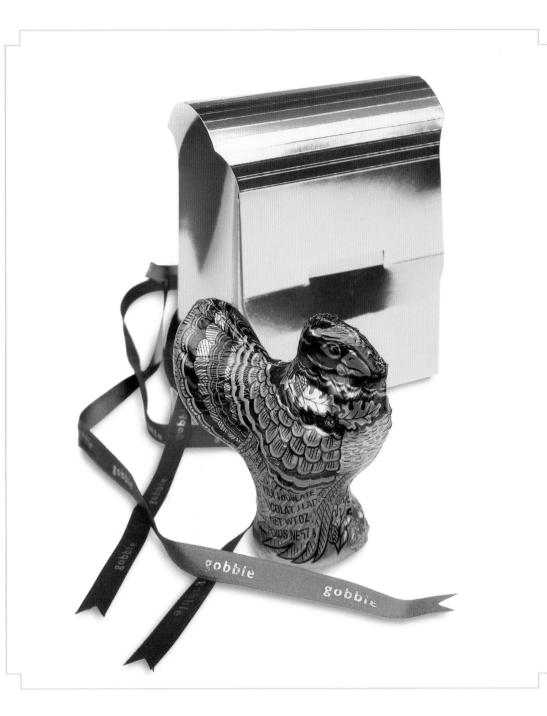

DESIGNER: Sutton Cooper

PROJECT: Festive mailing

DESCRIPTION: This mailer is comprised of a chocolate foil-wrapped chicken, packaged in a gold, cardboard roll-top box.

215

216

DESIGNER: Nick Clark Design

PROJECT: Festive mailing

DESCRIPTION: These self-promotional Christmas greetings come packaged in custom-made card boxes. The gifts within carry humorous messages.

DESIGNER: Cento Per Cento

PROJECT: Festive mailing

DESCRIPTION: Cento Per Cento wanted to convey the feelings of peace and love to their clients with these custom-made pieces.

217

218

DESIGNER: Four IV

PROJECT: Fashion show invitation for Mulberry

DESCRIPTION: A scroll of chocolate brown suede was screen-printed in gold with the dates, time, and venue of the show. The Mulberry name appears on a tag threaded around the rolled-up invitation.

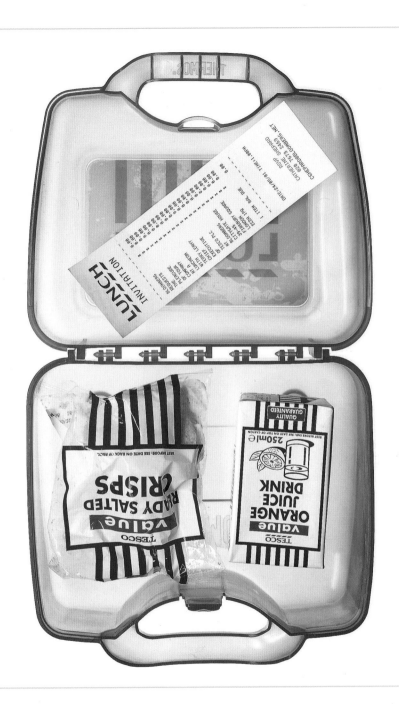

DESIGNER: Andrew Benson at Bloomberg

PROJECT: Tesco business lunch invitation

DESCRIPTION: This invitation takes the form of a supermarket receipt. The packaging consists of a clear plastic box with a branded sticker on the outside, and with some sample Tesco food products inside.

MERRY **CHRISTMAS**
XMAS 00
❄ FROM ALL AT **BIGGARTDONA**

HAPPY NEW YEAR
NY 01

220

DESIGNER: BD Tank

PROJECT: Festive mailing

DESCRIPTION: These inflatable mailings contain hand-finished gift boxes, each one with a chocolate inside. The inflatable bag has been screen-printed with a festive greeting.

DESIGNER: Graphic Partners

PROJECT: Festive mailing

DESCRIPTION: Graphic Partners wanted to convey the message that the thought behind something is the most important thing. Their solution was to send novelty socks with the label: "It's the thought that counts."

221

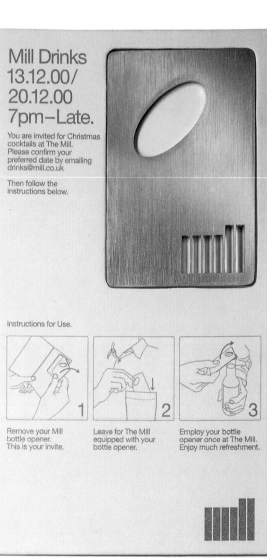

Mill Drinks
13.12.00/
20.12.00
7pm–Late.

You are invited for Christmas
cocktails at The Mill.
Please confirm your
preferred date by emailing
drinks@mill.co.uk

Then follow the
instructions below.

Instructions for Use.

1. Remove your Mill
bottle opener.
This is your invite.

2. Leave for The Mill
equipped with your
bottle opener.

3. Employ your bottle
opener once at The Mill.
Enjoy much refreshment.

222

DESIGNER: Made Thought

PROJECT: The Mill Christmas party invitation

DESCRIPTION: Enclosed in this invitation is a cardboard insert with a bespoke detachable stainless-steel bottle opener. Three humorous diagrams depict the "instructions" for the party.

INVITATION

20.04.94 - 04.30 PM

HEATHROW AIRPORT &
PUBLIC ART DEVELOPMENT TRUST

INVITATION

to the opening event of three
installations by Irish artists

Photography installation:
MICK O'KELLY

Light installation:
LOUISE WALSH

Sound installation:
MAURICE O'CONNELL

At Pier 4A, Terminal 1
Heathrow Airport

Opening event:

20.04.94 - 04.30 PM

For security reasons we ask you
to arrive by 4.15 pm.

DESIGNER: Mette Heinz at Atelier Works

PROJECT: Invitation to an exhibition of Irish artists at London's Heathrow Airport

DESCRIPTION: This invitation mimics the format of the old-style British passport. It was produced using a dark, royal blue card for the cover, with distinctive rounded cut-out windows.

223

what counts?

counting down to **2002**
Ten wishes from your friends at Methodologie

10

9

8

7

6

5

4

3

2

I

224

DESIGNER: Methodologie

PROJECT: Festive mailing

DESCRIPTION: These 11 card discs come neatly packaged in a round silver tin. They deliver a neat typographic countdown into the new year.

DESIGNER: Bureau Gras

PROJECT: Festive mailing

DESCRIPTION: Bureau Gras decided to send their clients and friends a card in the form of a packet of Christmas tree seeds. These came in a small plastic bag, along with a card.

225

226

DESIGNER: Pere Alvaro at Bis

PROJECT: Invitation for book launch

DESCRIPTION: This invitation takes the form of a mini version of the book being launched. The final piece was presented in the format of a color proof, folded twice like a form and mounted in the book.

As a place which caught our interest
AUSTRALIA
ranked about level with Belarus
and Barundi. Put in its
crudest terms, Australia was
slightly more important
to us in 1997 than
B A N A N A S
I MADE THIS IN YOUR HONOUR
When the Chinese when vows and affections failing
government recently took the decision to extend the teaching of English to nine-year-olds, they estimated that they would need to recruit
your soul leapt like a heron an additional one million English-teachers.
IN CRICKET MAD
from the salt, island grass into another India
HEAVEN
ubiquitous satellite TV
has made Geoffrey
Boycott one of the
greatest influences on
CONTEMPORARY INDIAN ENGLISH

1 Introduction / America: Melvyn Bragg 1.03
2 Plimoth Plantation: Mistress Standish! 2:37
3 Plimoth Plantation: Scott Attwood 2.17
4 Bill Bryson 8.16
5 School class learning English 1.48
6 William Labov 4.37
7 Professor Anna Zemtella 3.45
8 India Melvyn Bragg 00.42
9 Rudrangshu Mukherjee 4.23

As a place which caught our interest
AUSTRALIA
ranked about level with Belarus
and Barundi. Among the general
subjects which outstripped it were ballonet and
balloonist, the Church of Scientology, dogs (though
not dog sledding), Barneys, Inc., and Pamela
Harriman... Put in its crudest terms, Australia was
slightly more important to us in 1997 than
BANANAS but not nearly as important as ice cream.

I MADE THIS IN YOUR HONOUR
When the Chinese when vows and affections failing
government recently took the decision to extend the teaching of English to nine-year-olds, they estimated that they would need to recruit
your soul leapt like a heron an additional one million English-teachers.
IN CRICKET MAD
from the salt, island grass into another India
HEAVEN
ubiquitous satellite TV
has made Geoffrey
Boycott one of the
greatest influences on
CONTEMPORARY INDIAN ENGLISH

DESIGNER: Blast

PROJECT: Invitation to radio station party

DESCRIPTION: This invitation comes with an audio CD containing extracts from some of the radio station's shows. Both the CD and the invitation feature the same typographic devices.

'Holiday-wish-bambi' brought to you by H&K Creative

228

DESIGNER: Bisqit

PROJECT: Greetings card

DESCRIPTION: With a bit of pushing and folding, this card folds into a cartoon shape to sit on a desk.

DESIGNER: Fibre

PROJECT: Motorola invitation

DESCRIPTION: This invitation to the private viewing of an exhibition about portable, personal communication, was created in the shape and size of one of the earliest cellphones.

229

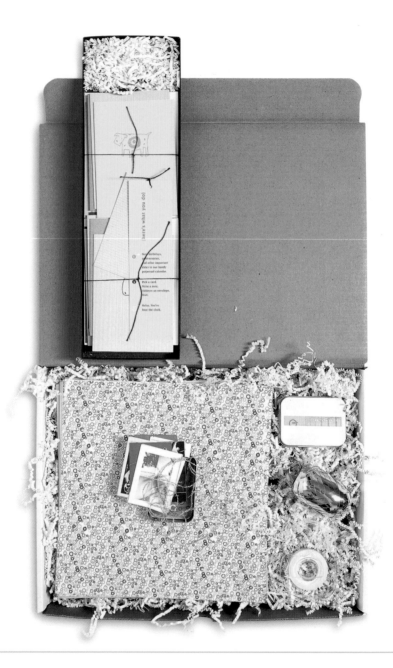

230

DESIGNER: KBDA

PROJECT: Festive mailing

DESCRIPTION: KBDA have found that the best promotions are gifts that people can use. This cardboard box comes full of gift wrap, sticky tape, ribbons, and gift tags suitable for all occasions.

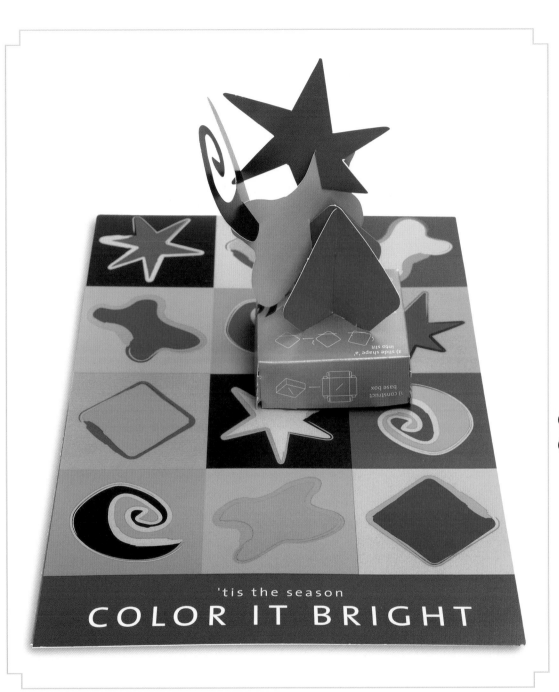

DESIGNER: FRCH Design Worldwide

PROJECT: Festive greetings card

DESCRIPTION: This holiday card consists of push-out card pieces that can be constructed into a sculpture that can remain on the recipient's desk for a whole year.

231

232

DESIGNER: Zuan Club

PROJECT: Promotional mailer

DESCRIPTION: This promotional mailer for the fifth anniversary of the Tokyo Design Center is cut, folded, and pasted to create a three-dimensional paper skyline.

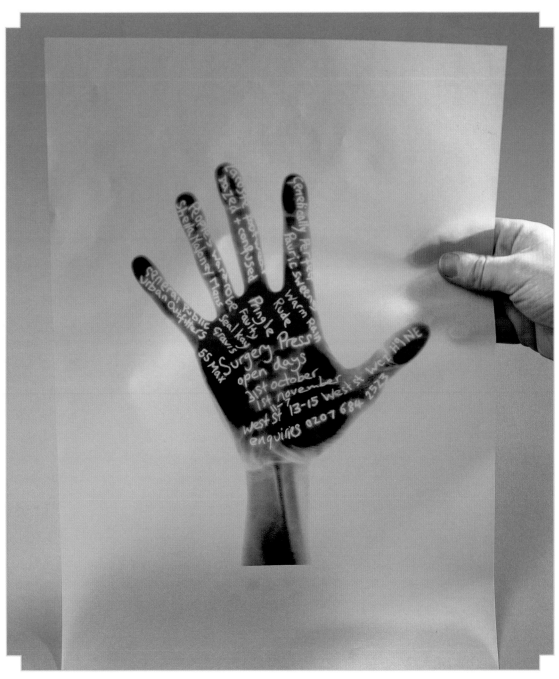

DESIGNER: Warm Rain

PROJECT: Invitation to a PR company's open day

DESCRIPTION: The transparency of the paper used to create this invitation really adds authenticity to the x-ray effect of the hand image.

233

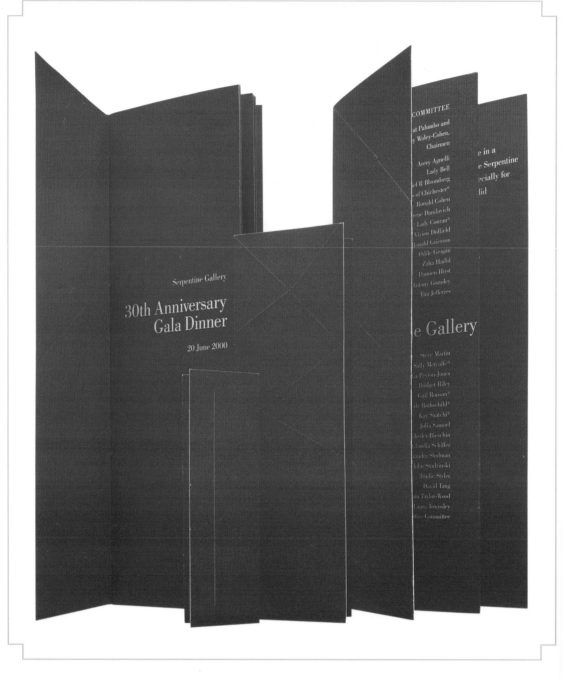

234

DESIGNER: Vince Frost

PROJECT: Serpentine Gallery 30th anniversary dinner invitation

DESCRIPTION: This invitation is split into four sections: the main invitation; an admission card; a place card; and a list of guests, patrons, and donors.

DESIGNER: Katherine Doubleday at Michael Nash

PROJECT: Alexander McQueen's Paris catwalk show invitation

DESCRIPTION: This invitation was designed to resemble a school exercise book, complete with drawings, scribbles, and doodles. Litho-printed stock with random ink marks helped to create the effect.

235

236

DESIGNER: Zen Design Group

PROJECT: Festive mailing

DESCRIPTION: This packaging company decided to show their design expertise by sending their clients this neat origami horse.

DESIGNER: Field Design Consultants Ltd.

PROJECT: Seasonal mailer

DESCRIPTION: This seasonal mailer was designed to direct people to the design consultancy's website. The stylish, but practical mittens were vacuum-sealed and mailed out to all potential clients.

237

238

DESIGNER: Blast

PROJECT: Press launch invitation for Pretty Polly and Playtex

DESCRIPTION: This invitation is printed onto pattern-cutting material with wording in the style of pattern instructions. The admission ticket is screen-printed onto silk, which is cut with pinking shears.

DESIGNER: Claire Kinge at Bloomberg

PROJECT: Invitation for British Council party at the Venice Biennale

DESCRIPTION: A survival kit for guests was the idea behind this invitation for a special party organized on the deserted island of Lazzaretto Nuovo. The bag holds a selection of essential survival items.

239

240

DESIGNER: Crescent Lodge Design

PROJECT: End of year greeting

DESCRIPTION: Two different end of year greetings from Crescent Lodge Design.
Both are simple, memorable, and playful ideas.

DESIGNER: Ralph Selby Associates

PROJECT: Festive mailings

DESCRIPTION: Each year Ralph Selby Associates send out a tree to their clients and friends. Each one is different and always constructed from a new material.

241

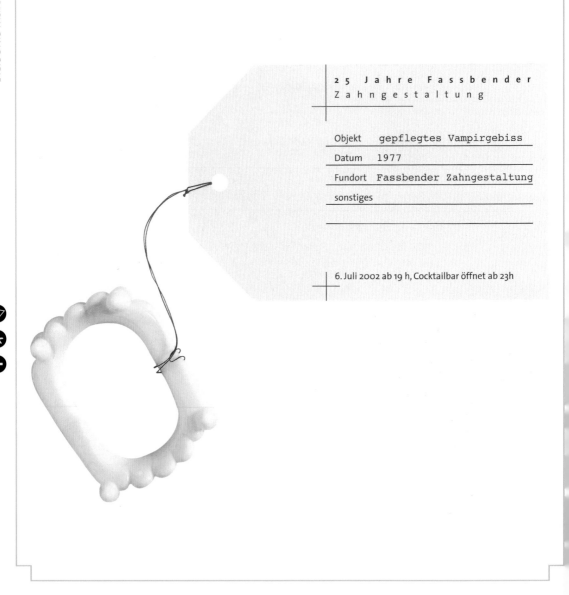

25 Jahre Fassbender Zahngestaltung

Objekt	gepflegtes Vampirgebiss
Datum	1977
Fundort	Fassbender Zahngestaltung
sonstiges	

6. Juli 2002 ab 19 h, Cocktailbar öffnet ab 23h

242

DESIGNER: Simon Gallus and Barbara Bättig at Fons Hickmann m23

PROJECT: Dentist studio's anniversary party invitation

DESCRIPTION: A plastic set of Dracula-style teeth was the response mechanism for an invitation to a dentist studio's vampire-themed cocktail party.

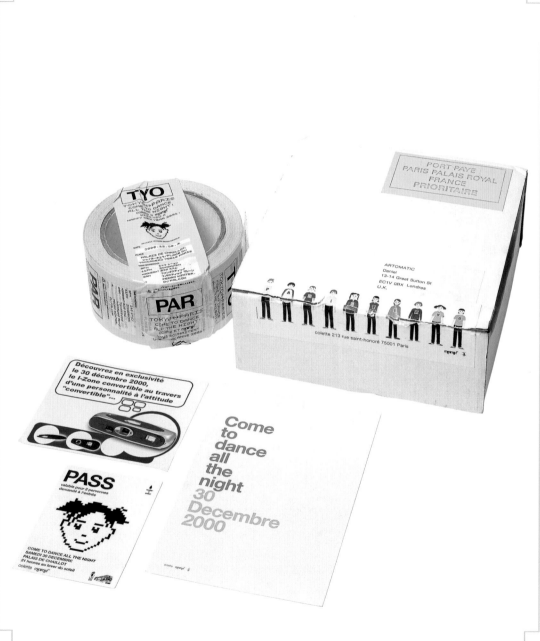

DESIGNER: Groovisions

PROJECT: Colette's New Year's Eve party invitation

DESCRIPTION: A corrugated cardboard box contains a combination of items for the event. Inside, the invitation is printed onto a roll of yellow packing tape while a pass card is printed in water-reactive ink.

Scott Witham
Deadline 21
25 Calderwood Road
Rutherglen
Glasgow
Scotland
G73 3HD

244

DESIGNER: Name

PROJECT: Festive mailing

DESCRIPTION: Created as a series of 12, each mailout contained a novelty gift, a motto, and a hat. Each set was vacuum-packed and mailed with an address label and stamp on the reverse.

apart giavischa in sonor
e dultschin nadal plein
bienas, bunas ed autras
carinadads per tgierp
ed olma. cordial engrazia-
ment per la fritgeivla
collaboraziun.

DESIGNER: Apart

PROJECT: Festive mailing

DESCRIPTION: Each of the employees at Apart designed their own wrapper for a gift box of candies that were mailed out to their clients and friends.

245

246

DESIGNER: Elmwood

PROJECT: Mailer for tree-planting campaign

DESCRIPTION: This mailer consisted of a tree sapling that recipients could personally plant in a forest. Details of the event and a response mechanism were also enclosed.

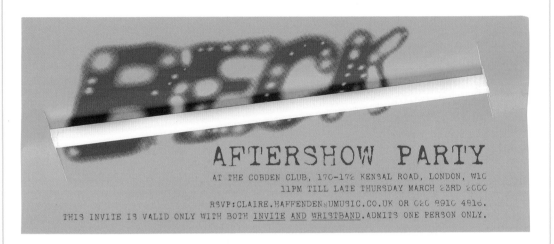

DESIGNER: Orla Quirke at Polydor

PROJECT: Party invitation

DESCRIPTION: A screen-printed, Day-Glo green card bearing a luminescent bracelet was designed by Orla Quirke for the singer Beck's aftershow party.

247

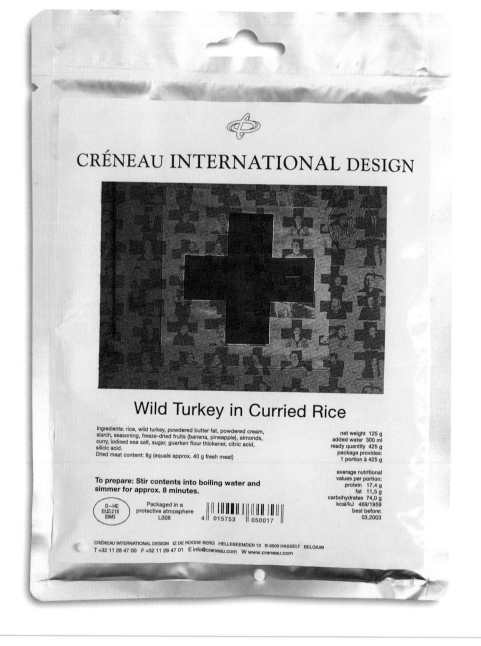

DESIGNER: Créneau International

PROJECT: Festive mailing

DESCRIPTION: Créneau International sent these vacuum-packed, ready-made meals to each of their clients and friends. The packs were branded with the company's name and logo.

a cynically transparent sales message

Happy Christmas from Thirdperson.

a genuine message of seasonal goodwill

DESIGNER: Thirdperson

PROJECT: Festive mailing

DESCRIPTION: This festive mailing cleverly uses two different colored trace papers to reveal two different messages. One is a seasonal greeting, the other a sales message.

249

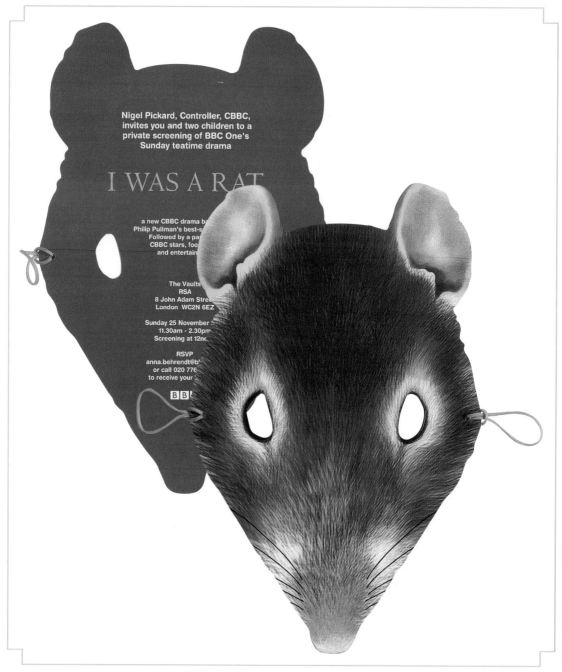

Nigel Pickard, Controller, CBBC,
invites you and two children to a
private screening of BBC One's
Sunday teatime drama

I WAS A RAT

a new CBBC drama b
Philip Pullman's best-s
Followed by a pa
CBBC stars, foo
and entertai

The Vaults
RSA
8 John Adam Stree
London WC2N 6EZ

Sunday 25 November
11.30am - 2.30pm
Screening at 12nc

RSVP
anna.behrendt@b
or call 020 776
to receive your

B B

250

DESIGNER: Blast

PROJECT: Invitation for launch party of *I Was a Rat*

DESCRIPTION: This invitation to the launch of a children's television series was made as a wearable mask. It was litho-printed and die-cut to the shape of a rat's face. Elastic was attached to hold the mask in place.

DESIGNER: Love

PROJECT: Wedding invitation

DESCRIPTION: This romance "novel" is a facsimile where the pages are left blank and a footnote announces that the happy couple's story is yet to be written. The contents page lists the wedding day's events.

252

DESIGNER: Staticreative Design Studio

PROJECT: Festive mailing

DESCRIPTION: This bottle of wine went out to friends and clients of Staticreative, with a set of personalized labels that the recipient could attach themselves.

Merry Christmas and a Happy New Year.

INSTRUCTIONS

FIG. 01 BUILD SNOWMAN.
Hat and scarf optional.

FIG. 02 ADD BUTTONS.
Place buttons as shown in illustration.

FIG. 03 ATTACH NOSE.
Attach cone here.

CONTENTS

x 6

x 1

BEST BEFORE END
WINTER 2002

Vanilla Design 3/2 Canada Court 81 Miller Street Glasgow G1 1EB 0141 204 0782 info@vanilladesign.co.uk www.vanilladesign.co.uk

DESIGNER: Vanilla Design

PROJECT: Festive mailing

DESCRIPTION: Six buttons and one ice-cream cone, neatly packaged in a slickly designed bag, make up this promotional "instant snowman" kit.

253

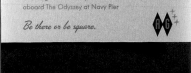

Anthony
and
Grace's
Wedding

WE'VE BEEN MARRIED FOR SO LONG,
IT'S ABOUT TIME WE ...

tied
the *knot!*

PLEASE JOIN US AS WE CELEBRATE
OUR 10TH ANNIVERSARY
WITH THE WEDDING WE NEVER HAD.

Monday, the nineteenth of August
Two thousand and two
at ten o'clock in the morning

Saint Ita Catholic Church
5500 North Broadway Avenue
Chicago, Illinois

Luncheon cruise reception
following the ceremony
aboard The Odyssey at Navy Pier

Be there or be square.

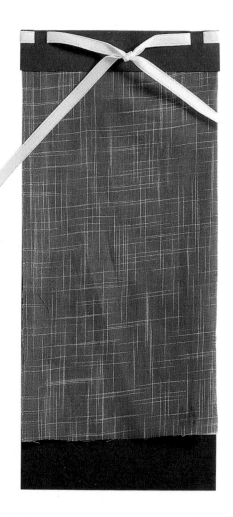

254

DESIGNER: Graceland Creative

PROJECT: Wedding invitation

DESCRIPTION: For this 1960s-themed wedding, a retro-inspired fabric was used as a top layer on the invitation to help set the tone of the event while piquing the guests' curiosity.

Letter: Derek Newark

Harold Pinter writes: It was a great shock to read of the death of Derek Newark (*obituary August 14*). I worked with him twice. He played Ajax in *The Trojan war will not take place* at the National and Roote in my play *The Hothouse* in the theatre and on television. He was a great comic actor. I have never laughed so much in my life as I did at the first reading of *The Hothouse* at Hampstead when his outraged exasperation with the crassness of those around him assumed monumental proportions. I also fell out of my seat at Ayckbourn's *Bedroom Farce* when the piece of furniture it had taken Derek ages to construct collapsed in front of him. The depth of his paralysed, pained disbelief was excruciatingly funny. It was a masterful demonstration of the essential gravity of farce. Offstage he could certainly be pretty rumbustious, "out of order," as he himself put it, but he was at core a gentle and generous man. I treasure his memory.

Birthdays

Ginger Baker, rock drummer, 59; Gordon Brand Jr, golfer, 40; Bill Clinton, US president, 52; Lord Cocks of Hartcliffe, former Labour chief whip, 69; John Deacon, guitarist and songwriter, 48; Mary Joe Fernandez, tennis player, 27; Dame Rose Heilbron, former high court judge, 84; Prof Sir David Hopwood, geneticist, 66; Richard Ingrams, editor, the Oldie, 61; Billy J Kramer, pop singer, 55; David Lodge, novelist, 77; the Rt Rev Dr Michael Nazir-Ali, Bishop of Rochester, 50; Dr Elizabeth Shore, former president, Medical Women's Federation, 71; Jill St John, actress, 58; Willie Shoemaker, former jockey, 67; John Mark Taylor, Conservative MP, 57; Henry Wyndham, chairman, Sotheby's, 45.

Please come to a celebration of Dad's life. Saturday 16th at 7pm foyer of the Royal National Theatre

DESIGNER: Quentin Newark at Atelier Works

PROJECT: Commemorative wake for Derek Newark

DESCRIPTION: Rather than create a simple invitation for their father's wake, Rohan and Quentin Newark decided to design and print a small book that strived to capture and celebrate their father's life.

Christmas
Stocking
2001.

256

DESIGNER: Duffy London

PROJECT: Festive mailing

DESCRIPTION: Two festive mailings created by Duffy London. One is a vacuum-packed Christmas stocking, filled with a mix of traditional and promotional items. The other is a branded sock.

DESIGNER: I.D. Designers

PROJECT: Festive mailing

DESCRIPTION: This do-it-yourself greetings card simply has the alphabet die-cut from a piece of thick card to create a stencil with which recipients can write their own message.

258

DESIGNER: Bloomberg

PROJECT: Party invitation

DESCRIPTION: This party invitation comes as two translucent films. Different elements of the information are viewed by looking at the invitation from both sides.

DESIGNER: Fake London

PROJECT: Fashion show invitation

DESCRIPTION: This invitation designed by fashion label Fake London's in-house team takes the form of a rosette. The rosette was mailed out in a simple plain envelope.

DESIGNER: Heard Design

PROJECT: Festive mailing

DESCRIPTION: Each team member at Heard Design was given 24 hours to come up with an image that reminded them of Christmas and New Year. These were then reproduced as a set of stickers.

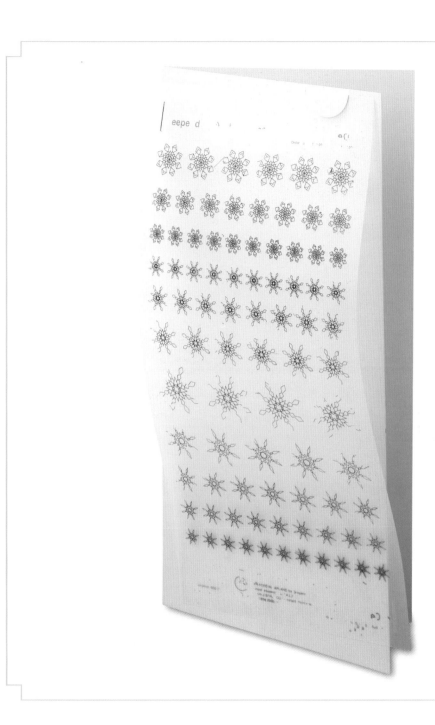

DESIGNER: De-construct

PROJECT: Festive mailing

DESCRIPTION: The idea behind this set of festive transfers is that each recipient can use them to make their own card or simply to give their paperwork a bit of sparkle.

261

262

DESIGNER: Vrontikis Design Office

PROJECT: Holiday mailer

DESCRIPTION: This greeting package arrives as an envelope of corrugated black card bound with a thin piece of red ribbon. Once opened, the centerpiece springs open with more exuberance than a cracker.

Concertina-folds in the middle are each cut with a single slit, and grasped in each of these is a selection of gift tags. Vrontikis Design Office sent this package of creative gift tags out to their clients and friends as holiday gifts. The tags contain an eclectic range of images collected from projects Vrontikis had worked on throughout the year.

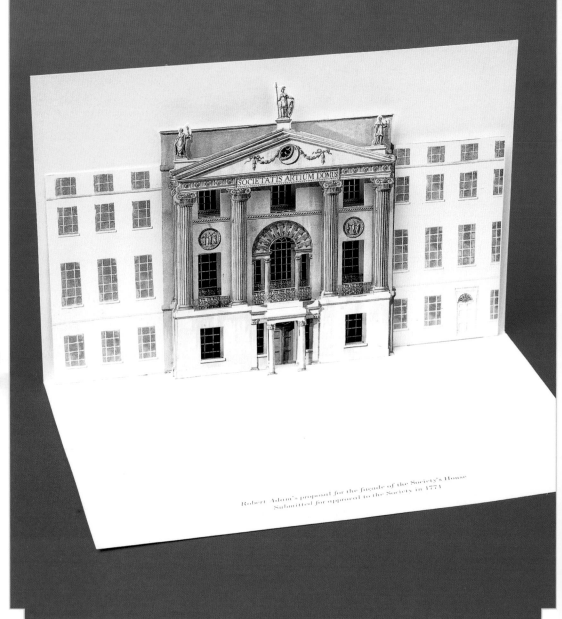

264

DESIGNER: Corina Fletcher

PROJECT: Royal Society of Arts Christmas card

DESCRIPTION: This pop-up card is based on an architectural drawing submitted to the Royal Society of Arts in 1771. The image pops up as the card is opened and sits like a three-dimensional model.

joy to the world

DESIGNER: Robert Sabuda

PROJECT: Christmas card

DESCRIPTION: This pop-up cathedral card includes an insert of colored plastic, which looks like a stained glass window when you put fairy lights behind it.

265

266

DESIGNER: Mytton Williams

PROJECT: Self-promotional mailer

DESCRIPTION: This mailer establishes the style of punning that is used in the rest of Mytton Williams' work. Printed on top is an invitation to drop into Bath, the name of the city where the company is based.

DESIGNER: Propeller

PROJECT: Promotional mailer

DESCRIPTION: This glass bottle was packaged in a straw-lined wooden box, complete with opener and sent to marketing directors in the wine trade.

267

PRODUCTS

270

DESIGNER: Gentil Eckersley

PROJECT: Carefree packaging for Johnson & Johnson

DESCRIPTION: This box packaging for Johnson & Johnson features a range of contemporary fashion images that are changed regularly in line with emerging trends.

DESIGNER: Saturday

PROJECT: Liberty press box

DESCRIPTION: Luxury, handmade box, using a range of colored and printed papers, cards, and ribbons. The text is foil-blocked on the box, and much of the imagery inside is screen-printed.

271

272

DESIGNER: Michael Nash Associates

PROJECT: John Galliano identity

DESCRIPTION: Created especially for this project, the newspaper—*The Galliano Gazette*—has been wrapped around a number of boxes and boldly branded with the the John Galliano logo.

DESIGNER: Michael Nash Associates

PROJECT: John Galliano identity

DESCRIPTION: As with the designs on the facing page, the John Galliano identity is applied to a number of different shaped and styled bags.

273

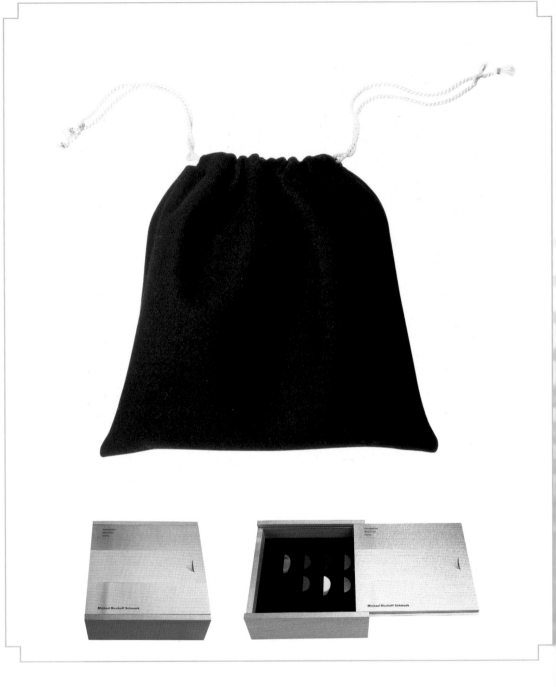

274

DESIGNER: Michael Bischoff Schmuck and hdr design

PROJECT: Jewelry packaging

DESCRIPTION: Presented in a drawstring black felt bag is a beautifully crafted wooden box. The box lid slides to reveal eight rings set in a sheet of high-density black foam.

DESIGNER: Michael Bischoff Schmuck and hdr design

PROJECT: Ring packaging

DESCRIPTION: The ring is placed within a recessed slot between two 100mm-square blocks of high-density felt. The two halves are secured by elastic bands and housed inside a wooden U-shaped container.

275

276

DESIGNER: Prada in-house design team

PROJECT: Cosmetics packaging

DESCRIPTION: The outer carton packaging is made from Tyvek, which was laminated to folding boxboard. The box closes on the side with a thin magnetic strip.

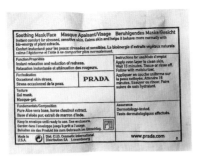

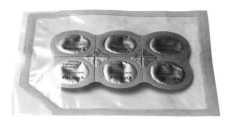

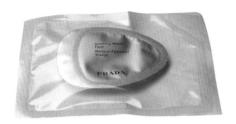

DESIGNER: Prada in-house design team

PROJECT: Cosmetics packaging

DESCRIPTION: Other Prada products come foil-covered in vacuum-formed trays, heat-sealed in tinted polyester film and Tyvek sachets, or in a range of small plastic tubes or bottles.

277

278

DESIGNER: Inventory

PROJECT: Burial Kit for the 21st Century

DESCRIPTION: Inventory were invited to design alternatives to traditional funereal artifacts. Their idea was this flexible PVC body bag. The black bags were screen-printed with white typography.

DESIGNER: Stanley Donwood

PROJECT: Promotional CD and video packaging for Radiohead

DESCRIPTION: This limited-edition promotional piece for the band Radiohead consists of a CD and video, packaged in a polystyrene box with a lift-off lid. The box comes in a padded bag, printed with song lyrics.

280

DESIGNER: Lindberg Optic Design

PROJECT: Glasses case

DESCRIPTION: Simplicity of form is employed in this glasses case. Two plastic or pearwood side panels are held in place by a sheet of sprung steel. The case gently springs open to reveal the glasses.

DESIGNER: Pentagram

PROJECT: Tretorn tennis ball packaging

DESCRIPTION: Pentagram decided to use a triangular shape for the packaging of these tennis balls.
The tube is produced in black polypropylene, with an embossed detail reflecting the "X" brand.

281

282

DESIGNER: Getty Images in-house design

PROJECT: Catalog packaging

DESCRIPTION: The use of expanded polystyrene packaging for this edition of the Getty Images catalog, lends itself to the glow-in-the-dark cover of the book.

DESIGNER: Gareth Hague

PROJECT: Cultural Ties packaging

DESCRIPTION: 150 ties designed by some of the world's leading contemporary artists were packaged neatly in these custom-made, routed foam tray boxes.

283

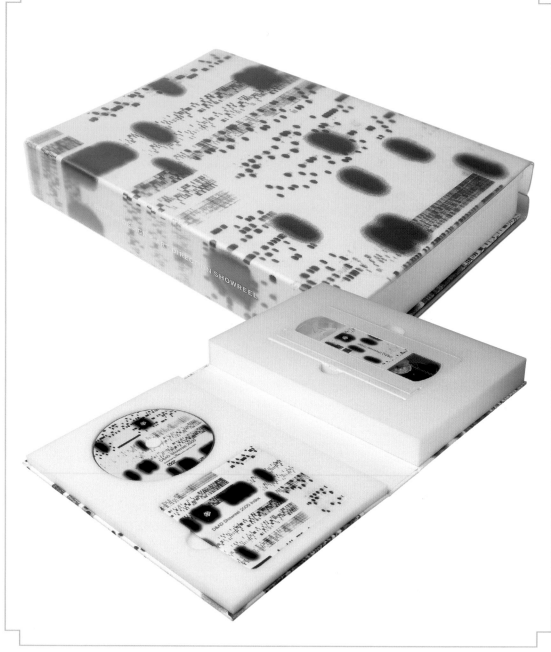

284

DESIGNER: Frost Design

PROJECT: D&AD annual showreel

DESCRIPTION: The showreel is housed in a white, high-density foam box along with a small brochure. The natural flexible sleeve that slides over the top echoes the dust jacket on the printed annual.

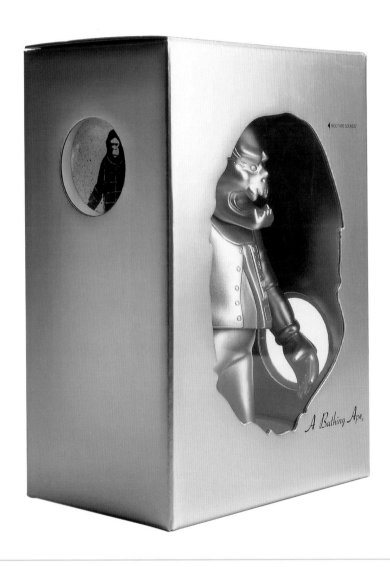

DESIGNER: Futura

PROJECT: Toy packaging for Bathing Ape

DESCRIPTION: The outer packaging is constructed from corrugated cardboard that has been die-cut to reveal the contents. The die-cut shape is a coded reference to the Bathing Ape company logo.

286

DESIGNER: Nick Crosbie

PROJECT: Dip-molded PVC book packaging

DESCRIPTION: A dip-molding process was used to create this unusual PVC slipcase. It is waxy and squeaky to the touch, but looks cold and steely.

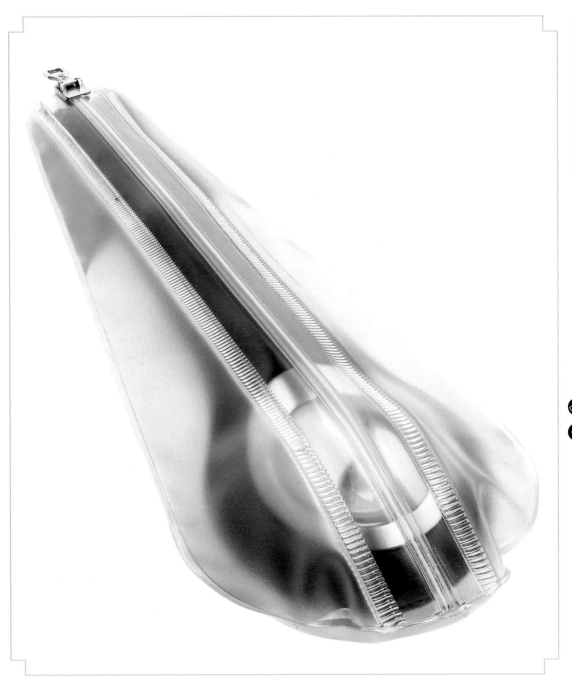

DESIGNER: The Boa Watch

PROJECT: Boa watch packaging

DESCRIPTION: The shape of this watch dictated the overall form of its packaging. The biomorphic shape and the materials that are used are completely removed from any other style of watch packaging.

287

288

DESIGNER: Marc Atlan

PROJECT: Perfume packaging for Comme des Garçons Parfums

DESCRIPTION: The dominance of the color red gives these printed vacuum-sealed bags a feel of exotic luxury.

DESIGNER: Marc Atlan

PROJECT: Perfume packaging for Comme des Garçons Parfums

DESCRIPTION: The printed vacuum-sealed bag emphasizes the exclusivity of this object by listing the few places from which it is available.

290

DESIGNER: 21st Century State-of-the-Art Packaging

PROJECT: Cigarette packaging

DESCRIPTION: The brushed aluminum finish, the hinged-lid closure, the way the metal has been rolled to create a shape more like jewelry or watch packaging, all make this cigarette box pure luxury.

DESIGNER: F. Bortolani and E. Righi

PROJECT: Shower gel packaging

DESCRIPTION: Packaged in a simple corrugated-card hinged box, this unusual shower gel dispenser is an interesting appropriation of a medical blood transfusion bag for domestic usage.

291

DESIGNER: North

PROJECT: Invitation to Ikepod watches exhibition stand

DESCRIPTION: Disguised as a package, this invitation was made using folding matte-laminated boxboard. The exhibition information appears on every surface, encouraging the user to explore the package.

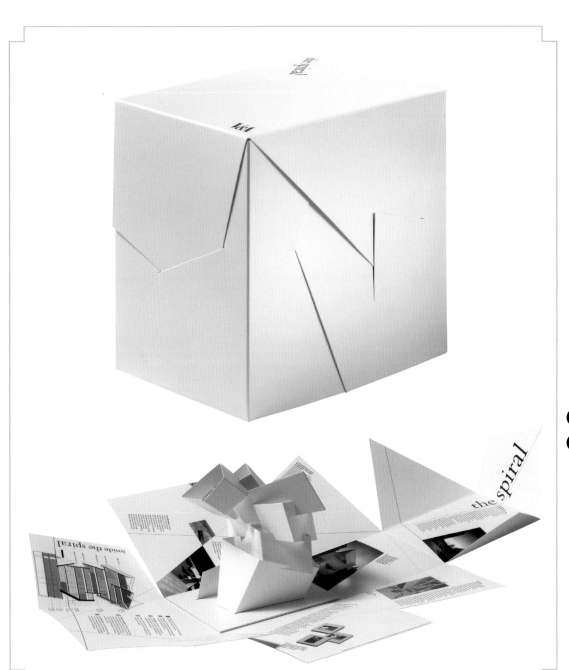

DESIGNER: Michael Johnson and Luke Gifford at Johnson Banks

PROJECT: Inform Project V&A Box

DESCRIPTION: Promotional, three-dimensional brochure for the proposed V&A building extension designed by the German architect, Daniel Libeskind.

293

294

DESIGNER: zoviet*france

PROJECT: Sleeve packaging for Red Rhino Records

DESCRIPTION: This record sleeve is constructed from sheets of acid-free tissue paper, screen-printed, and folded to size. It has a white PVC screen-printed insert.

DESIGNER: zoviet*france

PROJECT: Sleeve packaging for Red Rhino Records

DESCRIPTION: This record sleeve is constructed from two sheets of hardboard. It has been screen-printed, drilled, and fastened together with hand-dyed twine.

295

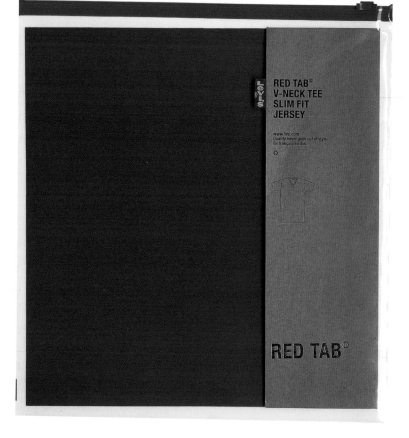

296

DESIGNER: Farrow Design

PROJECT: Levi's T-shirt packaging

DESCRIPTION: This T-shirt is packaged in a zip-lock bag with a card inserted and folded around the contents, falling short of total coverage in order to show the garment.

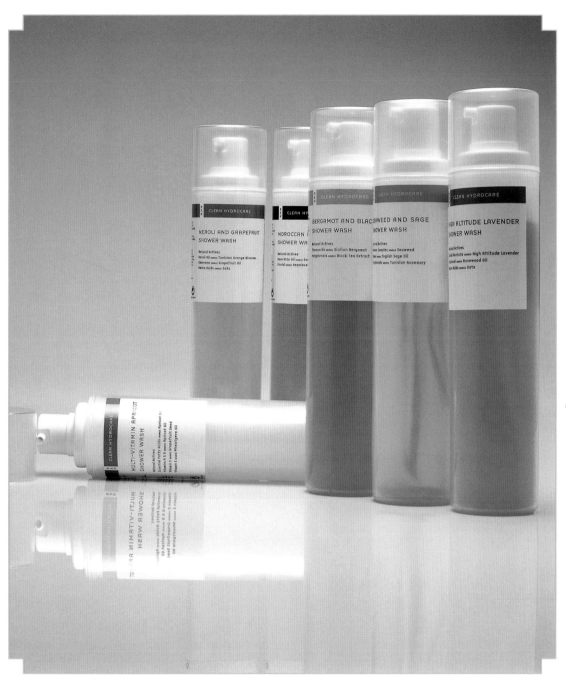

CLEAN HYDROCARE

NEROLI AND GRAPEFRUIT
SHOWER WASH

Natural Actives
Neroli Oil source Tunisian Orange Blossom
Limonene source Grapefruit Oil
Amino Acids source Oats

CLEAN HYDRO

MOROCCAN
SHOWER WA

Natural Actives
Rose Otto Oil source Da
Linalol source Nepalese

CLEAN HYDROCARE

BERGAMOT AND BLACK
SHOWER WASH

Natural Actives
Flavonoids source Sicilian Bergamot
Polyphenols source Black Tea Extract

CLEAN HYDROCARE

SEAWEED AND SAGE
SHOWER WASH

Natural Actives
Trace Complex source Seaweed
Thujone source English Sage Oil

CLEAN HYDROCARE

HIGH ALTITUDE LAVENDER
SHOWER WASH

Natural Actives
High Acetate source High Altitude Lavender
Terpenol source Rosewood Oil
Amino Acids source Oats

CLEAN HYDROCARE

MULTI-VITAMIN APRICOT
SHOWER WASH

Natural Actives
Essential Fatty Acids source Apricot Oil
Vitamins A & B source Apricot Oil
Vitamin E source Grapefruit Seed
Vitamin E source Wheatgerm Oil

DESIGNER: Ren

PROJECT: Beauty product packaging

DESCRIPTION: The packaging of this range of facial washes is clean, clear, and simple. The color coding of the upper section clearly identifies the individual products.

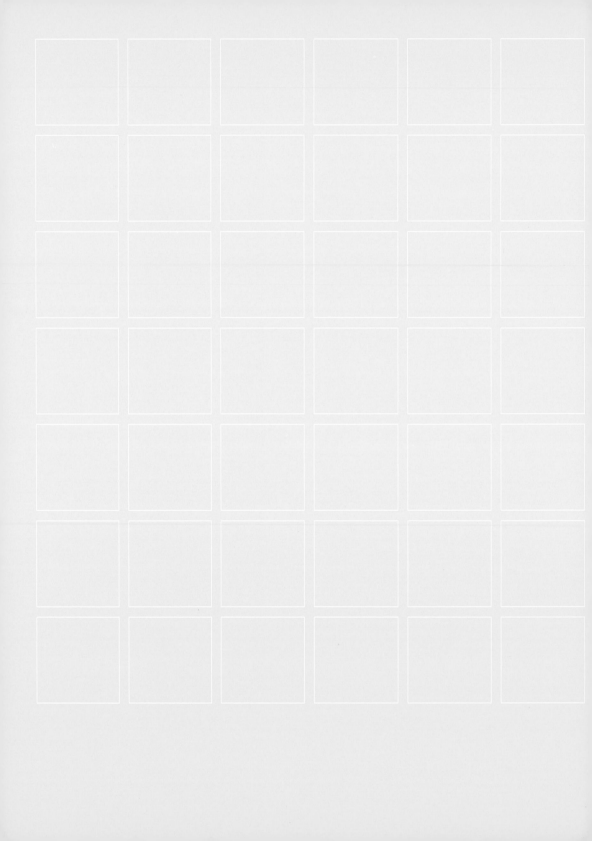

INDEX